SWISS COOKING

Dear Oneta & Johnny,
   The Rostis are
good — but the Cheese
Rostis are better!
   Merry Christmas 1986
          Love,

   Henry and Martha

By the same author

A TREASURY OF AUSTRALIAN COOKING

SWISS
COOKING

ANNE MASON

ANDRE DEUTSCH

FIRST PUBLISHED JUNE 1964 BY
ANDRE DEUTSCH LIMITED
105 GREAT RUSSELL STREET
LONDON WC1

COPYRIGHT © 1964 BY ANNE MASON
SECOND IMPRESSION APRIL 1970
THIRD IMPRESSION APRIL 1973
FOURTH IMPRESSION (REVISED) SEPTEMBER 1977
FIRST PAPERBACK EDITION MARCH 1982
SECOND IMPRESSION AUGUST 1983
THIRD IMPRESSION MARCH 1985

PRINTED AND BOUND IN GREAT BRITAIN
BY BILLING AND SONS LIMITED, WORCESTER

HARDBACK ISBN 0 233 96257 3

PAPERBACK ISBN 0 233 97494 6

CONTENTS

MEASUREMENTS

Although 1 kilogram (kg) equals a little less than $2\frac{1}{4}$ lb the Metrication Board has recommended the use of 25 grammes (g) for 1 oz as the standard unit, and although 1 litre (l) is a little more than $1\frac{3}{4}$ pints, we should calculate 125 millilitres (ml) to $\frac{1}{4}$ pint.

These measures will give a slightly smaller finished product but recipes will be simpler to convert.

25 g	replaces 1 oz
100 g	replaces 4 oz
500 g	($\frac{1}{2}$ kilo) replaces 1 lb
125 ml	replaces $\frac{1}{4}$ pint
250 ml	replaces $\frac{1}{2}$ pint
500 ml	($\frac{1}{2}$ litre) replaces 1 pint

TABLE OF COMPARATIVE TEMPERATURES

C	F	Gas mark
70	150	$\frac{1}{4}$
80	175	$\frac{1}{4}$
100	200	$\frac{1}{2}$
110	225	$\frac{1}{2}$
130	250	1
140	275	1
150	300	2
170	325	3
180	350	4
190	375	5
200	400	6
220	425	7
230	450	8
240	475	8
250	500	9
270	525	9
290	550	9

For me, Switzerland is a land of infinite variety in weather, scenery, people, language and food – and so much more interesting because of it.

A comparatively small country, it has much to offer both the casual visitor and the intending resident, from sun-bathed lakes and vineyards to snow-covered mountains, from delightful little villages still off the beaten track of the tourist, to cosmopolitan cities with their international attractions. It has four languages, German, French, Italian and Raeto-Romansch, and a cuisine embodying dishes inspired by the countries on its borders, adapted to the tastes and needs of the Swiss people.

In writing of Swiss cooking I am generally referring to the dishes to be found in Swiss homes rather than in restaurants and hotels, although many of these can also be enjoyed in restaurants which serve local specialities. Most of these recipes stem from country dishes, some of them centuries old, but as popular today as ever, even when made by housewives who live in cities and towns with all modern conveniences and a much wider choice of ingredients than the original cooks ever dreamed of.

It is interesting to note how each Canton or district has its own regional dishes – sometimes because of a plentitude of good local products such as a particular kind of cheese

9

or a lake well-filled with fish, and sometimes because
of its nearness to another country from which it has
taken ways of cooking its own natural specialities.

In choosing these recipes I have used those which can
be made by English housewives with ingredients readily
available in England. With this in mind I have not
mentioned such dishes as the celebrated Bündnerfleisch,
the air-dried meat which is such a speciality of several
districts, and which is served in delicious paper-thin
slices as an appetiser. Nor have I included the numerous
types of sausage which are made all over the country,
nor the enormous open fruit pies made by village housewives in Neuchâtel, and then taken to the local baker
for him to bake in his large bread-oven. I am sure you
would enjoy the pies, but I doubt if your local baker
would put them in his oven for you.

I would like to thank all those people who were so
generous with their culinary secrets, enabling me to pass
on to you these recipes; and those tourist officers all
over Switzerland who were helpful in my search for
typical recipes. My thanks also to Mr Fred Birmann, of
the Swiss National Tourist Office, Zürich, for his help
and encouragement; to Mr A. Kunz, General Mana-
ger of the Swiss National Tourist Office, London,
and to Mr Jürg Schmid, of the same office, who kindly
assisted me in translating the names of dishes. I would
also like to thank the Union Suisse du Commerce de
Fromage SA; the Swiss Processed Gruyère Cheese
Bureau; Knorr Soup Company; Mr E. Bonvin, former
London representative of the Swiss Wine Growers'
Association; and Swissair – whose yard-long menu is
the most attractive I have seen, and whose chefs were
generous with their recipes.

Along with Swiss foods there are also good Swiss wines, and the variety of these will probably surprise the British tourist who has not seen many Swiss labels in wine-stores at home. Many of the Swiss wines are at their best when enjoyed in their own country, although a number of excellent Swiss wines are now available in limited quantities in England.

Switzerland has 25,000 acres of vineyards, but it is in the French-speaking regions that the vine is most important. The largest producers of wines are the Cantons of Vaud, Valais, and Neuchâtel, and wines from these districts are sold throughout the country as well as being exported.

The produce of the Ticino (Tessin), Geneva, and Eastern and Central Swiss vineyards is mostly consumed locally, and the visitor to these regions should look for some of the local wines to enjoy while he is there.

Geneva wines are mostly light white wines produced from Chasselas stock, slightly dry, fresh and sometimes sparkling. The rather more harsh wines of the Ticino are known as Nostrano, and a strong fruity red wine, Merlot, is marketed under the label of Viti. From villages around the Lake of Zürich come rather sweet red wines such as Erlenbach, and a good Malvoisie is produced near Schaffhausen, on the Rhine.

Vineyards were established in many parts of Switzerland as far back as Roman days, when it was discovered that the climatic conditions of such regions as Valais, especially along the right bank of the Upper Rhône, were ideal for vines.

The best known and most popular of Valais wines is Fendant, a rather heady white wine of delicious bouquet. Dôle, the red wine of the region is sometimes considered by connoisseurs the best of Swiss wines. Vin du Glacier, a well flavoured white, is another locally produced wine worth trying.

The white Neuchâtel wines are light and sparkling, very refreshing when taken either with a meal or just for a drink with friends. The criterion of a good Neuchâtel vintage is that it forms a star in the glass as it is poured out, and has a real sparkle in the glass.

All along the sunny, south-facing shores of Lake Geneva to the east and west of Lausanne, terraced vineyards can be seen. The vintages from the east of Lausanne are known as Lavaux, while those from the west are La Cote. They are mostly white wines of good quality.

The City of Lausanne owns the famous 'Clos des Abbayes' and 'Clos des Moines', but these wines are never available to the public, being reserved for official municipal receptions. I must say it is always a pleasure to be a guest of the municipality.

As in all branches of agriculture in Switzerland, the vine-grower cultivates his land on a small scale. Terraces are models of energetic cultivation, with the idea of making the greatest use of every available space, and have usually been handed down through generations of sturdy husbandmen. Larger producers own their own equipment, presses, vinification and bottling plants, while smaller landowners press their harvest in communal presses and store the vintage in ancient vats in the family vaults.

During the months of September and October (depending on the weather) many of the wine producing areas hold annual vintage festivals, which are most interesting and amusing for the visitor. The vintage sales take place in November, and merchants and hoteliers come from all parts of Switzerland and from other countries to bid for the year's harvest.

Visitors to the French-speaking part of Switzerland can enjoy the good draught wines by asking for *vin du pays* and in the German section by asking for *offene Weine*. During the Autumn all over the country you will see many cafés and inns displaying a sign *Sauser*. This is not a sign for a new sauce or sausage, but indicates that the new season's wine, which has not yet fermented, is available inside. It is well worth trying if you want a refreshing drink which is claimed to be non-intoxicating (I have my doubts) and is certainly inexpensive.

Another non-alcoholic drink is grapillon, a white grape juice which must be served very cold, and a very good non-alcoholic apple juice known as sussmost or apfelsaft is on sale everywhere.

The famous kirsch, distilled from cherry kernels, comes from the cherry-growing district of Zug, and also from Lucerne, Basle and Schwyz. As well as being a very potent spirit, kirsch is an essential addition to fondue (*see* page 62) as well as a number of other Swiss dishes.

But I must disagree with one of my favourite authors, George Mikes, who tells you in his most amusing book,

Switzerland for Beginners (published by André Deutsch), that 'the Swiss love putting kirsch in everything they eat, particularly their soups'. On the other hand I certainly agree with him in his praise of Swiss soups and sausages – both are excellent, as you will find when you visit this lovely country.

The canton of Vaud stretching from Geneva to the Valais above the Lake of Geneva is one of the most important wine regions in Switzerland with vines covering the slopes running down to the lake.

Vevey has been the centre of viticulture in the Vaud since the Middle Ages, and from that time a wine-growers' festival has been held there four or five times each century, featuring splendid processions and pageants with casts of thousands.

Historically the festival can be traced back to a sort of quality control of the vineyards, followed by the awarding of prizes to the best local wine growers.

Today there are still tastings of local wines held all through festival time. The next Fête des Vignerons in Vevey will take place in July and August, 1977, but even at times when there is no festival Vevey is a place worth visiting to taste the wines of the prolific vineyards of the area.

POTATO SOUP
(PUSCHLAVER KARTOFFELSUPPE)

This is a recipe from Puschlav, or Poschiavo, a valley in the Grisons.

2 *lbs potatoes*
fat
1 *large onion*
1 *tablespoon flour*

2 *tablespoons fresh marjoram*
1 *cup milk*
3 *pints boiling water*
salt

Peel potatoes and cut into small cubes. Fry in smoking hot fat until pale golden on all sides, then add chopped onion and fry until transparent and just turning colour. Blend in flour. Add boiling, salted water, stirring until well blended, then simmer, covered, for about 40 minutes. Ten minutes before end of cooking time add finely chopped marjoram and stir in milk. Re-heat and serve at once.

15

CABBAGE SOUP

1 *large onion, chopped*   salt and pepper
2 *tablespoons butter or bacon fat*   *pinch dried thyme*
1 *small white turnip, shredded*   ½ *cup sour cream*
1 *lb cabbage, shredded*   4 *cups hot bouillon*

Melt half the butter in a large saucepan and cook onion until transparent, but do not brown. Add remainder of butter with cabbage and turnip and toss in the butter for 3 minutes over medium heat. Cover with bouillon (may be made with soup cubes), season to taste, add thyme and bring to boil. Cook slowly for 15 minutes, covered. Do not overcook, as cabbage should still have a little crispness left when served.

Divide between 6 soup bowls and top each with a spoonful of sour cream.

MINESTRONE

This recipe comes from the Ascona region. It is similar to the well-known Italian thick soup, and is almost a meal by itself.

1 *cup white haricot beans*   1 *small tin tomato paste or*
1 *clove of garlic*   2 *or 3 peeled tomatoes*
1 *large onion*   *sprig of rosemary*
2 *dessertspoons lard or bacon fat*   ½ *cup macaroni or other*
2 *or 3 carrots*   *pasta*
vegetables as required   2 *pints water*
   (*e.g. beans, cabbage, cauliflower,* *chopped parsley*
   peas, spinach)   *grated Sbrinz cheese*

Soak haricot beans in cold water overnight. Chop onion and garlic and cook for few minutes in hot fat, using a large saucepan. Add roughly chopped vegetables, haricot beans and water in which they were soaked, chopped tomatoes or tomato paste, rosemary, water, salt and pepper to taste. Simmer all together for 1 hour. Ten minutes before end of cooking time add macaroni and continue cooking. Serve sprinkled with grated cheese. To serve 4.

TRIPE SOUP
(BUSECCA)

During the winter this tripe soup is a typical part of a meal in the Ticino part of Switzerland, where veal tripe is used more often than the ox tripe we are familiar with in England. But if the ox tripe is well cooked when you buy it from the butcher it is quite suitable for this soup.

1 *lb tripe*	1 *tablespoon haricot beans*
¼ *lb fat bacon*	*(pre-soaked)*
1 *onion, chopped*	3–4 *tomatoes, sliced*
1 *clove of garlic, chopped*	*diced potatoes*
1 *carrot, sliced*	*grated cheese*
1 *stalk of celery, sliced*	*salt and pepper*
1 *tablespoon chopped parsley*	

Cut the bacon into dice and fry until crisp, and the fat has been rendered from it. Cut tripe in thin strips and brown lightly in the bacon fat, then add onion, garlic, carrot, celery, parsley and tomatoes, toss in the fat, then cover pan and steam for a few minutes. Add beans and 3 pints water, cover and simmer for 1½ hours. Add the diced potatoes 20 minutes before end of cooking time.

Serve with grated cheese sprinkled over each plateful.

CONSOMMÉ CELESTINE

3 *pints beef or chicken consommé*   about ⅛ *pint milk*
2 *eggs, separated*   *oil or butter*
pinch salt   *chopped chives*
4 *oz plain flour*

The plain consommé is garnished with strips of pan-cakes for this excellent soup, which is usually served on festive occasions by the housewives of Zürich. The pancakes are best made only very shortly before serving, or they are tough.

Sift flour and salt into a basin and beat in egg yolks, then the milk. Stand for 15 minutes. Beat egg whites until stiff and fold into batter. Grease a thick frying pan and drop in one tablespoon of batter at a time, tilting pan in all directions to spread batter very thinly. Fry on one side for 2 or 3 minutes or until cooked through and golden. Turn out of pan on to a board and cut into thin strips, like noodles. Continue until you have sufficient pancake strips for 6 serves. Drop into hot consommé and sprinkle each serve with chives. Grated cheese may be sprinkled over the soup instead of chives.

ZUPPA ALLA CAVALOTTA

An easy-to-prepare soup which is almost a meal by itself, as served in the Locarno district.

slices of stale bread   *chopped onion*
slices of cheese   *bouillon*
butter

Amounts depend on numbers to be served. Put alternate layers of bread and cheese in a soup tureen, the last layer to be bread. Cook onion in butter until soft and golden then pour over top of bread in tureen. Pour enough boiling bouillon over the layers to cover them generously, and stand for several minutes before serving.

GRAVY SOUP

This is a speciality of Basle.

5 tablespoons butter or chicken fat	7 cups stock
	1 cup croûtons
5 tablespoons flour	¼ cup grated Gruyère cheese

Melt the fat in a deep saucepan, then blend in the flour until smooth. Cook over low heat until flour has browned, stirring continuously until desired colour. Gradually stir in the stock, stirring until mixture boils. Cover and cook over moderate heat for 1½ hours, stirring occasionally. Taste for seasoning. Serve with croûtons and sprinkle each serve with grated cheese.

CUCUMBER SOUP
(POTAGE CONCOMBRE)

1 medium size cucumber	3 pints beef bouillon
2 dessertspoons cornflour	butter
1 egg yolk	salt and pepper

Peel and cut cucumber into slices and cook in a little butter in a covered pan for a few minutes, then add ½ cup water and simmer until tender. Add bouillon (made with cubes if necessary) bring to boil, then stir in corn-flour blended to a paste with a little water or bouillon. Stir until slightly thickened, then cook for 5 minutes. Remove from heat and quickly stir in beaten egg yolk.

CREAMED ONION SOUP

3 *tablespoons butter*
3 *tablespoons flour*
3 *cups milk (or 2 cups milk and*
  1 cup vegetable stock)
1 *large onion, sliced*

salt and pepper
½ *teaspoon French mustard*
extra butter
grated cheese

Melt butter in saucepan and stir in flour until smooth. Gradually stir in milk, or milk and stock, stirring until the mixture boils and thickens, then cook over very low heat for about 5 minutes, stirring occasionally. Heat a little extra butter in a small pan and fry the onion, turning to cook on all sides until transparent and pale golden. Add to soup and season to taste. Serve at once, sprinkled with grated cheese. To serve 4.

VEGETABLE AND CHEESE SOUP

2 *carrots*
1 *medium onion*
1 *stalk of celery*
3 *dessertspoons butter*
1 *oz flour*

2 *pints water or stock*
8 *oz grated cheese*
2 *cups milk*
salt and pepper
chopped parsley or croûtons

Peel and chop carrots and onion very small, and chop the celery, including the leaves. Melt butter in a large saucepan and sauté the vegetables until onion is transparent. Blend in the flour, then stir in water or stock, stirring all the time until boiling and slightly thickened. Cook for 15 minutes, then add cheese and stir until it melts, then add milk, continuing to stir until it is nearly boiling. Taste for salt and pepper. Serve at once with either parsley or croûtons.

POTATO AND CHEESE SOUP

4 medium potatoes, peeled and
    sliced
4 oz grated Sbrinz cheese
1½ pints water
1 tablespoon flour
1 tablespoon butter

1½ cups milk
salt and pepper
pinch dried marjoram
1 egg yolk (optional)
croûtons

Cook potatoes in the water until quite tender, then press through a sieve with the water. Melt butter in a fair-size saucepan and blend in flour, cooking for a few minutes. Stir in potatoes and water and bring to boil, stirring all the time, then cook for 10 minutes, stirring at intervals. Mix cheese and milk and stir into soup, cooking until cheese is melted. Taste for seasoning, remove from heat and stir in beaten yolk if using. Serve at once with croûtons.

URI CHEESE SOUP

On his arrival in Altdorf, chief town of the Uri Canton, one of the first things any visitor is shown is the statue of a large, bearded warrior with a crossbow on his shoulder, and a small boy at his side. This of course, indicates that we are in the home-town of the famous character, William Tell, one of the greatest heroes of Switzerland.

And if you are there for a meal, you will certainly be encouraged to try one of the specialities of the region, this cheese soup which has an unusual addition in caraway seeds.

3½ oz grated Emmentaler cheese
1 tablespoon butter
4 tablespoons flour
1 quart cold water
1 cup hot milk

1 heaped tablespoon
   caraway seeds
salt, pepper, nutmeg
1 clove of garlic
   (optional)

Melt the butter in a large saucepan, and stir in the flour, allowing to brown slightly. Take saucepan away from heat, and with lid of saucepan in one hand, pour the cold water quickly over the browned flour, covering instantly with the lid. After a minute add the caraway seeds, and stir well, then simmer over low heat for 15 to 20 minutes. Season to taste. A clove of garlic may be added while soup simmers, then removed before serving. Stir grated cheese into hot milk in a soup tureen, then pour soup over the milk. Give it a stir and serve at once.

BEAN AND BEEF SOUP

This hearty and nourishing soup comes from the Grisons Canton, and it is particularly suitable for people who live in this mountainous region, with its hard winters.

You may have difficulty in finding the Grisons Canton on some maps, as there are three versions of the name: Grisons is the French name, Graubunden is the German one, and in the ancient Romanch language it is Grischun. The inhabitants speak a mixture of German, Italian and Romanch, and as there are many excellent tourist resorts such as St Moritz, Davos, Klosters and Chur in this region, English is also widely spoken.

There are a number of very good soups served in this canton, often with the local bread which is made from ground corn and barley flours, and in the more remote areas you will see ovens attached to the outside of houses where the bread is baked for each family.

5 *pints water*
1½ *lb shin of beef*
1 *meaty ham bone (uncooked)*
1 *onion spiked with cloves*

3 *oz barley*
3 *oz dried white beans*
1 *teaspoon salt*
½ *bay leaf*

Wash barley and beans and soak overnight in water to cover. Next day make up amount of water as required, add ham and seasonings and bring to boiling point. Add beef, cover and simmer together for 3 hours.

The meat can be served separately as another course with vegetables.

BOMBOLINES

These are delicious additions to bouillon or clear soup,
either chicken or beef flavoured, and are usually served
for special occasions.

1 *dessertspoon butter*	2 *eggs*
2½ *pints water*	4 *oz mortadella sausage*
1 *cup plain flour*	*salt to taste*
2 *oz grated Emmental cheese*	*fat for frying*

Bring water to boil and add butter. When melted add
flour and stir until it resembles a thick paste and leaves
the sides of the pan clean. Add eggs and grated cheese
and beat well. Chop mortadella into small pieces and
add. Have deep fat very hot. Drop small pieces of the
paste into the hot fat and fry until puffed and golden.
Drain well on absorbent paper.

These can be prepared the day before and added to
bouillon at the last minute before serving.

SOUP WITH AN EGG

A popular combination of bouillon (either beef or
chicken) with egg makes a good beginning for a meal,
or it makes almost a light meal by itself.

For each serve fry a slice of bread in butter until
golden on both sides and place in a soup plate. Heat the
bouillon in a shallow pan and poach required number
of eggs (one for each serve). Carefully lift poached egg
and place on fried bread, then pour 1½ cups bouillon
over the egg on toast. Sprinkle with grated cheese and
serve at once.

ANCHOVY EGGS

Set in the mountainous border country of Switzerland and Italy the lovely lakes of Lugano, Como and Maggiore attract many visitors each year. Here the food has a strong Italian influence, a delicious contrast to the no less interesting German-inspired food of the North. This luncheon salad is a tasty example.

6 *hard-boiled eggs*
1 *lb tomatoes, peeled*
salt and pepper to taste

1 *small tin anchovy fillets*
lettuce leaves
mayonnaise

Cut eggs in halves lengthwise and scoop out yolks, pressing through a sieve into a basin. Cut 1 large tomato in halves and scoop out seeds, then chop the flesh very small. Chop three anchovy fillets and add with tomato to egg yolks. Blend well together, adding a little of the anchovy oil if mixture is too stiff, and season to taste. Fill egg whites with mixture and arrange on lettuce leaves. Garnish with tomato slices and remaining anchovy fillets. Serve mayonnaise separately.

SALADE DE TILSIT

Another tasty salad from the same region.

Line a salad bowl with crisp lettuce leaves. Cut Tilsit cheese into cubes and add to a good rich mayonnaise, with capers to your taste. Pile on the lettuce and garnish with rolled fillets of anchovies. Add a sprinkle of freshly ground black pepper just before serving.

ONION AND TOMATO SALAD

As the onions in this salad are marinated for about 3 hours, it is not one which can be put together in a hurry, but it is worth the time for making.

2 *fairly large onions*	*salt and pepper*
3 *tablespoons olive oil*	1 *clove of garlic*
1 *tablespoon wine vinegar*	*(may be omitted)*
2 *tablespoons dry red wine*	3 *large tomatoes*
¼ *teaspoon dry mustard*	*lettuce leaves*
½ *teaspoon sugar*	

Slice onions into rings, separate and place in deep bowl. Place oil, vinegar, wine, mustard, sugar, salt, pepper and garlic in a small jar and shake well to blend. Pour over the onion rings, cover and stand for 3 or 4 hours, spooning marinade over onions several times. Fifteen minutes before serving, slice tomatoes into the bowl with onions and spoon dressing over them. Cover and chill. When ready to serve lift tomato slices carefully out with a slotted spoon and arrange in a circle on a chilled salad plate which has been lined with lettuce leaves.

Drain onion slices and arrange in the middle of the tomato ring.

The dressing remaining in the bowl can be strained and used to dress a plain lettuce salad next day.

MIXED SALAD
(GEMISCHTER SALAT)

Serve as a side dish with fish or white meat.

Grate equal quantities of white radish or very young white turnip and young carrots and mix together. Add tops of very young spinach leaves, roughly chopped, and marinate in oil and vinegar dressing (see below) for 30 minutes before serving.

GREEN SALAD
(GRÜNER SALAT)

1 *head lettuce*
2 *heads chicory*
1 *tablespoon chopped parsley*
1 *tablespoon salad oil*
1 *tablespoon cider vinegar*
1 *teaspoon sugar*
salt and pepper

Wash lettuce and chicory well and dry thoroughly. Tear into pieces the desired size and place in salad bowl with parsley. Mix last four ingredients well and pour over salad. Toss leaves well and stand for a little time before serving.

APPENZELL SALAD
(SALADE APPENZELLOISE)

Cut Appenzell cheese and plain boiled potatoes into finger-size pieces and mix with mayonnaise or salad dressing. Arrange on crisp lettuce leaves and garnish with slices of cervelas sausage or cooked sliced frankfurters and sliced sweet gherkins.

SALAMI SALAD
(SALADE AU SALAMI)

Add chopped parsley, gherkins and capers to mayonnaise and stand for a little time. Cut Gruyère cheese into thin pieces and mix with equal amount of cooked and sliced green beans. Arrange on lettuce leaves and pour prepared mayonnaise over. Garnish with thin slices of salami sausage rolled into cones.

HUNTER'S SALAD
(SALADE CHASSEUR)

Cut Tilsit cheese, radishes and canned mushrooms into slices, using equal quantities of each. Add a little sour cream or yoghourt to mayonnaise, blending well, and serve over salad on lettuce leaves. Garnish with asparagus tips.

CHEESE SALAD
(SALADE AU FROMAGE)

To ½ cup mayonnaise or salad dressing add 1 teaspoon grated horseradish, 1 small onion chopped fine and a sprinkle of pepper and stand for a little time. Cut Gruyère or Emmental cheese into cubes and mix with sliced radishes and peeled, sliced tomatoes. Arrange on lettuce leaves and add prepared dressing.

'SWISS CREST' SALAD

This favourite salad comes from Valais, in the Rhône valley, where asparagus of the finest quality grows. The ham used is home-dried *jambon cru*, but in England ordinary cooked ham would be used.

2 *lb fresh, young asparagus*	4 *slices of ham*
½ *lb tomatoes*	*mayonnaise*

Wash and scrape asparagus and cook in salted water until tender. Drain well and cool. Divide into four equal portions and arrange on a large white plate to form a cross, with the tips all in the centre, but leaving a little space in the centre for mayonnaise. Fill gaps between arms of cross with 4 rolls of ham, then surround with slices of tomatoes.

SPINACH SALAD

Only very young spinach should be used for this salad.

½ *lb spinach*
1 *finely chopped onion*
salt, pepper, pinch sugar
2 *dessertspoons lemon juice*
3 *dessertspoons olive oil*

chopped parsley
chopped chives
2 *hard-boiled eggs*
red radishes, sliced

Wash spinach well and dry, patting with a clean cloth to remove moisture. Chop finely and mix with chopped onion, parsley and chives. Make dressing with lemon juice and oil, add seasonings and add to spinach mixture, tossing well. Garnish with eggs cut in quarters and sliced radishes.

BEETROOT SALAD

Arrange cooked, sliced beetroot on lettuce leaves, sprinkle lightly with finely chopped spring onions, and top each serve with a spoonful of sour cream or plain yoghurt.

ASPARAGUS AND CHEESE CASSEROLE
(ASPERGES À LA FROMAGE)

Excellent asparagus is grown in the Rhône valley, along with many kinds of vegetables and fruit, and this is a way of using asparagus as prepared in this region.

2 *lbs asparagus*	4 *oz grated cheese*
1 *oz butter*	*salt and pepper*

Wash the asparagus well and cut off the tough ends. Using a deep saucepan, place the asparagus, stems downward, in the pan and boil in salted water for 15 minutes, or until tender. Drain well, and cut in pieces about 1-inch long. Butter an oven-proof dish and place a layer of asparagus pieces on the bottom. Sprinkle with salt and pepper, grated cheese and small pieces of butter. Repeat these layers, finishing with a good layer of cheese on top. Dot with butter and put into a moderately hot oven (375 deg F or No 6) until cheese is bubbling and lightly browned on top. Serve at once.

Do not use a strongly flavoured cheese or you will spoil the flavour of the asparagus.

VEGETABLE CASSEROLE WITH CHEESE DUMPLINGS

Although this dish is served in many parts of the country, I enjoyed it first in Appenzell, and always associate it with that region. Here too, I tasted a number of different sausages which are a speciality of the north-eastern part of Switzerland.

Appenzell is a charming little town situated at the far end of a green valley, but it is memorable as the centre of a region where the women wear the loveliest national costume I have seen, many of the older ones coming to church on Sunday in their long coloured gowns with black bodices and ruched white epaulettes. Their winged headdresses are like huge butterflies, and they can be seen at their best at the annual festival of Corpus Christi.

But here is the casserole, which can be made with any vegetables in season.

¼ pint haricot beans	2 teaspoons chopped parsley
2 onions	2 peeled tomatoes
2 oz fat	½ pint stock
2 carrots	salt and pepper
2 stalks celery	

For the dumplings you need:

3 oz flour	pinch mixed herbs
½ teaspoon baking powder	salt and pepper to taste
1 oz grated cheese	milk and water to mix

Cover the washed beans with water and leave for 12 hours, then boil in water in which they were soaked, adding more water if necessary. Drain and if no stock is available, add a bouillon cube to the bean water.

Slice onions and fry in hot fat until golden brown, add sliced carrots and celery and fry gently until the fat is absorbed, but be careful they do not brown too much. Place in a greased casserole, add the beans, parsley and lastly the sliced tomatoes, seasoning to taste, then pour the stock over. Cover and cook in a moderate oven for 40 minutes.

Make the dumplings by combining the dry ingredients, then mixing to a soft dough with milk and water. Arrange small portions of the dough over the vegetables, and continue cooking for another 20 minutes or until dumplings are risen and cooked.

The casserole can be varied by adding any chopped left-over ham or meat to the vegetables.

MUSHROOM
AND MARJORAM PIE

This is one version of the famous mushroom dish served at Lucerne, called Kugelipastete. It can be made as a casserole, or covered with a lid of short pastry to serve as a pie.

1 *lb mushrooms*
1 *dessertspoon chopped marjoram*
1 *teaspoon chopped chives*
1 *teaspoon chopped parsley*
½ *cup chicken stock*
¼ *cup dry white wine*
½ *cup melted butter*
salt and pepper

Clean mushrooms, but do not peel unless necessary. Chop the stalks small, and slice mushrooms. Arrange in a buttered pie dish or casserole. Combine remainder of ingredients and pour over mushrooms, cover and bake in moderate oven (350 deg F or No 5) for 20 to 25 minutes.

If serving as a pie, cover with rolled out pastry, cut a few slits for steam to escape, brush over with milk or egg yolk and bake in moderately hot oven for 25 minutes or until pastry is golden.

TOMATO PIE
(PITZ)

A recipe from the Lower Valais.

short pastry
6 large ripe tomatoes
8 oz Gruyère cheese
2 medium onions

salt and pepper
1 teaspoon fresh mixed
  herbs, chopped
½ cup sour cream

Line a medium-size oblong baking dish with pastry. Cut tomatoes in halves (they should be ripe but firm) and scoop out the middles. Season with salt and pepper and turn upside-down to drain. Chop the cheese fairly small, chop the onions and mix cheese, onions and chopped herbs together. Fill tomatoes with this mixture, seasoning to taste. Pour the sour cream evenly over the tomatoes. Arrange them in the pastry-lined tin and bake in a hot oven (425 deg F or No 8) until pastry is golden and tomatoes are cooked.

Another version of this pie uses chopped cooked asparagus instead of onions as the filling for tomatoes, and uses chopped chives and parsley instead of other herbs.

HAM AND MUSHROOM TART
(GATEAU TESSINOIS)

10 oz flaky pastry	sprig of rosemary
6 oz cheese	2 eggs
4 oz ham, chopped	1 cup milk
1 small tin mushrooms	salt and pepper
(champignons)	pinch ground nutmeg

Line a large tart plate or sandwich tin with pastry. Arrange the drained mushrooms, ham, cubed cheese and rosemary on the pastry. Beat eggs and milk, add seasonings and pour over mixture in pastry. Bake in a moderate oven (350 deg F or No 5) 20–25 minutes until pastry case is cooked and filling is set. Serve hot.

ONION TART
(GATEAU AUX OIGNONS)

Gateau aux oignons is a typical dish of the Schaffhausen district, but it will be found in many other parts of the country as well.

Schaffhausen is the gateway to Switzerland from Germany. It is a picturesque town, situated on the Rhine, and dominated by the Castle of Munot perched on the hilltop overlooking the town. A visit to the spectacular Rhine Falls is an absolute 'must' for every visitor to this part of the country, as well as a taste of this delicious onion tart.

10 oz flaky pastry	2 eggs
2 lbs onions, sliced	1 cup top milk
lard or butter	salt and pepper

Line a large tart plate or sandwich tin with pastry. Cook the onions in lard or butter until transparent and slightly golden. Fill tart with onions, beat eggs and milk with seasonings and pour over onions. Bake in a moderate oven (350 deg F or No 5) until pastry case is cooked and filling is set.

If liked, some chopped bacon can be fried with the onions for the filling.

GREEN BEANS
(GRÜNE BOHNEN)

1 lb green beans
2 rashers lean bacon
1 tablespoon chopped onion
1 clove of garlic, chopped
1 tablespoon butter
salt and pepper

Top, tail and slice beans and cook in a little boiling salted water until tender, but not too soft. While beans are cooking fry onion, garlic and cubed bacon in butter until onion is golden brown and bacon is crisp. Drain beans well and toss lightly with bacon mixture. Season to taste and serve at once.

CREAMED GREEN BEANS

1 lb green beans
salt
1 dessertspoon butter
1 dessertspoon cream
1 teaspoon cornflour
pinch ground nutmeg
1 cup liquor from beans

Top, tail and slice beans and cook in a little boiling, salted water until tender, but not too soft. Drain and retain liquor, measuring 1 cupful into saucepan. Blend cornflour with a little water and stir into boiling bean liquor, stirring until thickened. Stir in nutmeg and cream, but do not allow to boil, remove from heat and stir in butter.

Beans may be added to sauce, or the sauce poured over each serve of beans on plate as desired.

SPINACH TART

6 *oz short pastry*   *salt, pepper and nutmeg*
1 *lb spinach*   3 *triangles Petit Gruyère*
2 *tablespoons butter*   6 *tablespoons thin cream*
2 *eggs*   5–6 *anchovy fillets*

Wash spinach well and remove tough stalks. Place in saucepan with butter, cover and cook until quite tender, stirring at intervals. When cooked, drain well and chop finely. Line a flan case or deep tart plate with pastry and place chopped spinach over the base of tart. Beat up eggs and cream (top milk may be used), season with salt, pepper and nutmeg to taste, but remember the anchovies are salted. Pour over the spinach. Cut each cheese triangle in half and arrange alternately with the anchovy fillets on top of tart. Bake for about 25 minutes in moderate oven (350 deg F or No 5). Serve hot or cold.

COUNTRY CABBAGE
(NEUCHÂTEL)
(CHOUX À LA PAYSANNE)

1 *firm cabbage*   1 *rasher of bacon*
2 *oz fat*   2 *lb potatoes*
1 *Neuchâteloise sausage* *salt*

Wash the cabbage well and cut in quarters. Melt the fat in a pan, add the cabbage and enough water to come ¼ way over the cabbage, salt and bacon. Cover and simmer for 30 minutes. Prick the sausage with a fork and add to cabbage with the peeled potatoes. Continue cooking for another hour.

Frankfurters could be used in this dish, which is served as a main meal.

LEEKS NEUCHÂTELOISE
(POIREAUX À LA NEUCHÂTELOISE)

1½ *lb leeks*   2 *tablespoons Neuchâtel*
½ *pint water, boiling*   *white wine*
salt to taste   1 *tablespoon flour*
                          ½ *lb liver sausage*

Trim and wash leeks and cut into ½-inch slices. Put into boiling, salted water and cook, covered for ½ hour. Add the liver sausage and simmer for 25 to 30 minutes. Remove the sausage. Blend the flour with the wine and stir into leeks, cooking for several minutes. There should not be much liquid left in saucepan before thickening.

This is also served as a main dish, adding the sausage after thickening.

BAKED MUSHROOMS
(GEBACKENE PILZE)

1 lb mushrooms
2 medium-size onions, chopped
2 oz butter
salt and pepper to taste

1 tablespoon flour
1 pint sour cream
chopped parsley

Peel mushrooms and cut in slices. Brown onions lightly in butter, add mushrooms and cook for 5 minutes, stirring once or twice. Transfer mushroom mixture to a buttered ovenproof dish, season with salt and pepper. Blend flour with sour cream and pour over mushrooms. Sprinkle with parsley. Cover and bake in a moderate oven (350 deg F or No 5) for about 30 minutes.

VEGETABLE RISOTTO
(LOCARNO)
(RISOTTO MIT GEMÜSE)

1 large onion, sliced
butter or oil
1 cup rice
salt and pepper

2 cups cooked vegetables
1 pint vegetable stock
3 or 4 ripe tomatoes
chopped parsley

A mixture of any available vegetables should be used for this recipe, e.g. green beans, peas, diced celery, diced carrots, diced green and red peppers, and they should all be cooked together in boiling salted water for 10 to 15 minutes or until tender. Save the water after draining the vegetables. Wash the rice well beforehand and dry.

Cook the onion in butter, or use half butter and half oil, in a fairly large thick pan. When onion is transparent add the rice and cook for 5 minutes, turning frequently with a fork. Add half the stock and simmer, uncovered, for 20 minutes, adding remainder of stock as it is absorbed. Stir in vegetables and chopped parsley, and peeled, diced tomatoes. Reheat for 3 or 4 minutes and serve at once.

Grated cheese may be served with this if desired.

BRAISED RED CABBAGE

This is good served with pork dishes, and goes well with pigs' trotters (page 87) as a change from sauerkraut.

small red cabbage (1–1½ lbs)	1 dessertspoon wine vinegar
1 onion	salt and pepper
1 cooking apple	2 tablespoons red wine or
1 tablespoon butter or lard	water if preferred
1 dessertspoon sugar	

Wash and drain cabbage, removing coarse outer leaves and core. With a sharp knife, cut into shreds. Chop onion finely; peel, core and chop apple. Heat fat in a large pan and lightly brown onion. Add cabbage and cook for a few minutes, turning frequently. Add remainder of ingredients, bring to boil and simmer, covered, for 45 minutes, or until cabbage is tender but still a little crisp and almost all the liquid has cooked away. Stir occasionally to prevent scorching.

This can be re-heated if desired. It is excellent with pork or game meat such as venison.

CREAMED SPINACH
(SPINAT MIT RAHM)

2 lb fresh young spinach
1 tablespoon butter
salt to taste
½ teaspoon sugar

2 tablespoons cream or
    top milk
pinch ground nutmeg

Wash spinach well in several waters, drain lightly and put into large saucepan, covered, for 5 or 6 minutes until wilted. Turn spinach several times while cooking. Drain well and chop very fine. Melt butter in thick pan and add spinach, with salt to taste. Sauté spinach, stirring frequently, until most of the moisture has evaporated. Stir in cream, sugar and nutmeg, mixing well, and heat without boiling. Serve at once.

CELERY ROOT WITH HAM

3 young celery roots
1½ oz butter
1½ oz flour
salt and pepper

1 cup milk
1 egg yolk
8 oz raw ham
lemon juice

Wash and trim celery roots and cook in boiling water until nearly tender. Cut in slices. Melt butter in pan and blend in flour, then stir in milk until smooth and thick. Remove from heat and add lightly beaten egg yolk, beating in lightly, then add ham cut in thin strips, celery slices, salt, pepper and enough lemon juice to flavour. Heat for a few minutes without allowing to boil. Serve over hot boiled rice.

ONIONS WITH RICE

1½ lb onions	salt and pepper
2 tablespoons butter	grated cheese
2 tablespoons water	boiled rice or spaghetti

Peel and slice onions about ¼-inch thick. Melt butter in a fairly large frying pan and add water, then arrange onion slices in an even layer. Season with salt and pepper. Cover and cook slowly until liquid evaporates and onions look transparent, shaking pan at intervals. Cook for another 5 minutes until just golden, then sprinkle thickly with grated cheese and put under hot griller until cheese is melted. Serve at once over hot boiled rice or spaghetti.

STUFFED TOMATOES (HOT)
(TOMATOES FARCIES, CHAUD)

6 firm, ripe tomatoes	1 egg
1 tablespoon soft breadcrumbs	½ cup milk
4 oz grated Emmental cheese	salt and pepper

Choose firm tomatoes as nearly the same size as possible. Cut a slice from the top of each and carefully scoop out the pulp, season the shell with salt and pepper and turn upside-down to drain. Beat the egg and milk together, add breadcrumbs and cheese and mix well. Fill tomatoes with this mixture, stand in a buttered baking dish and bake in a moderate oven for 10–15 minutes, or until tomatoes are tender and filling is cooked. Be careful tomatoes do not break with overcooking.

STUFFED TOMATOES (COLD)

6 *firm, ripe tomatoes*   1 *lb young peas*
salt and pepper   *mayonnaise*
1 *tablespoon lemon juice*   *mint or parsley*
3 *tablespoons olive oil*

Prepare tomatoes as in preceding recipe. Mix oil and lemon juice and paint insides of tomatoes with this dressing, using a pastry brush. Chill. Cook the peas in a little salted boiling water, drain well and cool. Mix with just enough mayonnaise to moisten, chill well then fill hollowed-out tomatoes. Garnish with a little sprig of parsley or mint.

Serve on lettuce leaves as a salad or to accompany cold chicken or veal.

RÖSTI
OR SWISS FRIED POTATOES

This is a very typical recipe which is served all over Switzerland, sometimes as an accompaniment to meat, or sometimes as a meatless meal. It is certainly not for those on a slimming diet!

6 *large potatoes*   1 *onion, finely chopped*
¼ *cup lard or butter*   *(optional)*
salt and pepper

Boil potatoes in their skins until tender, drain and peel immediately. Cut into thin slices. Heat the butter or lard in a large pan, add potatoes (and the onion if using), season with salt and pepper, and fry over good heat, turning the potatoes at intervals to brown on all sides. Now lower the heat, press the potatoes firmly into the pan and fry very slowly for a few minutes until a golden crust forms underneath. Turn out with the crust uppermost and serve at once.

RÖSTI WITH CHEESE
(ROSTI AU FROMAGE)

Another version of the popular rösti is made by coarsely grating the boiled, peeled potatoes and mixing with 2 oz grated Emmental or Gruyère cheese. A large chopped onion is fried until golden in butter and mixed with the potatoes. This mixture is packed into a well buttered cake tin and baked in a slow oven until browned. This is then turned out on a heatproof plate, more grated cheese is sprinkled over the top, and it is put under a hot grill or back in the oven just long enough to half-melt the cheese.

With a green salad and a cup of creamy coffee this makes an excellent meal.

POTATO AU GRATIN

There are many local variations of this popular potato dish, and I have tasted it made with the addition of sliced hard-boiled eggs between the potato layers; with chives used instead of onion, and as made in Schwyz with alternate layers of potatoes, cheese and thinly sliced apples.

6–8 *medium potatoes*	1 *small onion, chopped*
2 *oz butter*	1 *clove of garlic*
1 *egg*	4–5 *oz Gruyère cheese*
about 1 *pint milk*	*salt and pepper*

Peel and slice the potatoes and arrange in layers in a casserole which has been rubbed round with the cut clove of garlic. Sprinkle each layer with a little finely chopped onion and dot with pieces of butter. Grate the cheese and put 1 tablespoon aside, adding remainder to beaten egg. Season with salt and pepper. Warm the milk and add to cheese and egg mixture, then pour over potatoes. The milk should come just to top layer of potatoes, but not cover them. Sprinkle remainder of cheese over top. Bake in moderate oven (350 deg F or No 5) for 45 to 50 minutes or until potatoes are tender and top golden.

The cheese may be sliced thinly instead of grated.

ANCHOVY SAUCE FOR POTATOES

This is a tasty sauce to serve over large potatoes baked in their skins, or it can also be served over plain boiled rice.

6 oz processed Gruyère cheese   6 anchovy fillets
3 tablespoons milk   1 tablespoon chopped parsley
pepper

Chop the cheese fine and add to milk, stirring over low heat until cheese has melted. Add chopped anchovies and pepper and continue stirring until sauce is thick and smooth. Remove from stove and add parsley. Cut two slits crosswise on top of each potato, squeeze to open and pour sauce over top of each. Serve at once.

POTATOES
STUFFED WITH ANCHOVIES

Bake large, well-scrubbed potatoes in their skins for approximately 1 hour or until tender when pressed between the fingers. Cut a slice from the top of each potato and scoop out the pulp into a basin, adding butter, a little milk and a dash of pepper. Mash until smooth and creamy, but not too moist. Chop anchovy fillets (allowing one to each potato) and a few sprigs of parsley and add to potato pulp, blending well. Re-fill potato skins with pulp, place slices cut from tops back in position and bake in moderate oven just long enough to re-heat. Serve at once with salad for lunch or supper.

POTATO CAKE

There are a number of variations of this dish, which makes an excellent meatless meal. This one comes from the Zug district.

2 *lbs potatoes*   1 *egg*
8 *oz grated Gruyère cheese*   1 *pint milk*
salt and pepper   *butter*

Cook the potatoes in boiling, salted water until quite tender, drain and mash with a little butter until smooth and creamy. Grease an ovenproof casserole and put in half the potatoes, season with salt and pepper and sprinkle with half the cheese. Cover with another layer of potatoes and remainder of cheese. Beat egg and milk together and pour over potatoes and cheese. Dot with small pieces of butter and bake in a fairly hot oven until set and top is golden brown. Serve at once.

Half Gruyère and half Parmesan cheese can also be used.

Another version of this recipe, from Central Switzerland, replaces the cheese with thinly sliced apples, and omits the milk and egg; while yet another mixes mashed potatoes and stewed apples together and adds a couple of beaten eggs, then bakes the mixture in a casserole.

POTATO GNOCCHI

1 *lb potatoes*   1 *egg*
4 *oz flour*   2 *oz butter*
salt and pepper   *grated cheese*

Cook the potatoes until quite tender, drain, then rub through a sieve. Mix in the flour, beaten egg, ½ oz butter and season to taste. Knead into a smooth dough, roll out into finger-thickness rolls and cut into ¾-inch pieces. Have a large saucepan of boiling, salted water ready and drop the pieces a few at a time into the water so it does not go off the boil. Do not cook too many at one time. After about 3 minutes they should rise to the top of the water. Remove with a slotted spoon and place in a buttered ovenproof dish. When all the pieces are cooked sprinkle thickly with grated cheese and dot with remainder of butter. Place in a warm oven for a few minutes until cheese has melted, then serve at once.

Cooked, well-drained and chopped spinach can be added to the potato mixture for another version of this dish.

FISH

PIKE FROM LAKE OF ZUG

Giant pike from Zug are famed throughout Switzerland, but this recipe calls for one of 2 to 3 lbs. The fish should be scaled, cleaned and washed, soaked in salt water for 1 to 2 hours before cooking, then drained well and wiped dry.

2–3 lb pike	½ cup dry white wine
3 rashers bacon	2 oz butter
3–4 sage leaves	1 medium carrot
1 onion spiked with 2 whole cloves	salt and pepper
½ cup fish stock	2 dessertspoons cream
	1 teaspoon anchovy paste

Season inside of prepared fish with salt and pepper. Peel carrot and place inside fish with a strip of bacon. Place other rashers of bacon on the bottom of an oven-proof casserole large enough to take the whole fish, and arrange fish (back upwards) in casserole. Add sage, onion, stock and wine, and dot with small pieces of butter. Cover dish and bake in a moderate oven (350 deg F or No 5) for about 15 minutes, then uncover and continue cooking for 30 minutes, or until fish is a light gold, and cooked through. Baste fairly regularly with liquid in dish. When fish is cooked, carefully lift from casserole to a heated serving dish and keep hot while you make the sauce. If preferred, the liquid in the casserole can be drained off into a saucepan and the fish left in the baking dish to serve. If the fish is rather large this is sometimes easier. Strain the juices from the dish, adding a little more fish stock or water if necessary, blend in the anchovy paste and cream, re-heat slightly and add a few drops lemon juice. Serve with fish, which should be garnished with lemon slices. Plain boiled potatoes are best with this.

PERCH FILLETS À LA OUCHY

Ouchy is the lake-side suburb of Lausanne, on Lac Léman – or the Lake of Geneva, as it is usually called in England. Much favoured by visitors, it has many hotels and restaurants where excellent food is obtainable, and fish, fresh from the lake, is a popular dish.

Prepare the fish as described above, and fry in butter until golden. Remove from pan and keep hot. Make a sauce with $\frac{1}{2}$ oz butter, $\frac{1}{2}$ oz flour, salt and pepper and $\frac{1}{4}$ pint dry white wine. Add 2 or 3 peeled and chopped tomatoes and 2 or 3 tablespoons chopped fried mushrooms, and cook for a few minutes. Pour over fish and serve.

BLUE RIVER TROUT
(PETITES TRUITES DE RIVIÈRE AU BLEU)

For this dish choose small trout, which should for best results be killed immediately before they are to be cooked. Clean the fish but do not scale them or the famous blue colour will be spoilt. Have ready prepared a court bouillon (*see* page 55), place fish in an ovenproof dish and sprinkle with 2 tablespoons hot vinegar, then add enough hot court bouillon to cover. Cook in a moderate oven (350 deg F or No 5) for 5 or 6 minutes, or just tender. Be very careful not to overcook. Drain off stock in dish and serve at once, garnished with parsley and slices of lemon, with melted butter served separately.

Small carp can be cooked in the same manner, to turn blue like the trout.

FISH FILLETS, LUCERNE STYLE

The Lake of Lucerne is the home of a number of different kinds of fish, all of which are made into very appetising dishes by cooks in the neighbourhood. This is a very popular one.

2 *lb fish fillets*	1 *oz butter*
court bouillon for poaching fish	1 *oz flour*
cooked, sliced potatoes	*salt and pepper*
½ *pint mixed fish stock and*	½ *teaspoon dry mustard*
white wine	*grated cheese*

Cook fish in court bouillon until tender (*see* page 55), then drain and place side by side in a large buttered ovenproof dish. Arrange potato slices round (but not

over) the fish. Melt butter in saucepan and stir in flour
and mustard until smooth. Gradually add stock and
wine, stirring until it boils, then cook for 2 or 3 minutes
over low heat. Pour this sauce over fish and potatoes,
and top with a generous layer of grated cheese. Bake in
a moderate oven (350 deg F or No 5) for about 20
minutes, until sauce bubbles and turns golden.

PERCH FILLETS IN BEER

This is a simple and unusual way of cooking fish. The
fillets are soaked in beer for 45 minutes before cooking.
Then drain well, coat with seasoned flour and fry in
hot fat until golden on both sides. Serve at once with
squares of parsley-butter, and quarters of lemon.

FISH AND GRUYÈRE PIE

Any fine white fish may be used for this recipe, quantities depending on numbers to be served.

small fish fillets   *soft breadcrumbs*
butter   *salt and pepper*
processed Gruyère cheese

Butter an ovenproof casserole and sprinkle with breadcrumbs, salt and pepper. Arrange a layer of fish fillets
on breadcrumbs, dot lightly with butter, then sprinkle
with more breadcrumbs, salt and pepper, and cover
with a layer of sliced cheese. Repeat these layers once
again, finishing with layer of cheese. Bake in moderate
oven (350 deg F or No 5) for 30 to 35 minutes, or until
fish is cooked. If cheese browns too much on top, cover
with piece of buttered paper.

FISH PASTRY STICKS

These are best served hot, but they are very tasty when cold to take for a picnic. Allow 2 for each serve.

3 or 4 fillets of plaice   *salt and pepper*
6 oz processed Gruyère cheese   *1 lb short pastry*

Cut each fillet in halves lengthwise and season with salt and pepper. Roll pastry fairly thin and cut into rectangles about 3 inches by 5 inches. Cut cheese into fingers about ½ inch thick. Place a finger of cheese on each fillet and roll fish firmly round cheese. Place on pastry and roll up neatly (as you would for sausage rolls), leaving ends open. Place on a greased baking dish and bake in medium hot oven (400 deg F or No 6) until pastry is golden and fish is cooked through. Serve hot or cold with vegetables or salad.

FISH IN ENVELOPES
(POISSON EN ENVELOPES)

Any small fish may be used for these, such as whiting or fresh haddock, and they should be cleaned and filleted. Allow one fish per person, also 1 triangle of processed Gruyère cheese, dried basil or mixed herbs, salt and pepper, and squares of cooking foil, well buttered.

Season fillets well and place one fillet on each square of foil. Cut cheese triangles in halves through the middle and place the two pieces on top of fish. Arrange other fillet on top, then sprinkle with herbs very lightly. Fold foil securely all round like an envelope, place fish packets on oven tray and bake in moderate oven for 20 minutes, or until fish is tender.

Serve in the foil, but open tops of envelopes.

FISH RISOTTO

Any fairly coarse fish can be used for this recipe, which comes from the Lugano district. If fresh fish is not available, canned tuna or salmon can be used with good results.

whole fish, approx 1½ *lb*	*2 oz butter or margarine*
1 *cup rice*	*salt and pepper*
1 *large onion*	1 *pint fish stock*
1 *clove of garlic (optional)*	1 *tablespoon chopped*
1 *tablespoon chopped sweet red*	*parsley*
pepper (fresh or canned)	1 *bay leaf*

Clean and scale fish, place on rack or on a large square of butter muslin in fish boiler or saucepan with bay leaf, salt and enough water to cover well. Simmer gently for 20 to 30 minutes, or until fish is cooked well. Remove from pan and strain stock. Skin fish and flake the flesh, removing any bones. There should be 2 cups of flaked fish.

The rice should be well washed, drained well and dried in a clean tea towel some time before cooking. Chop the onion and fry in butter or margarine until soft but without colouring, stirring well. Add rice and cook until transparent. Pour in half the hot fish stock and bring quickly to boil, then continue cooking over low heat until rice is cooked, adding remainder of stock as necessary. Keep stirring at frequent intervals with a fork to prevent rice from sticking to pan. When rice is tender stir in fish, parsley and red pepper, seasoning to taste. Re-heat for a few minutes, then serve at once.

Grated cheese may be served separately with the risotto.   To serve 4.

FISH FILLETS WITH MUSHROOMS
(FILLETS DE POISSON AUX CHAMPIGNONS)

4 fillets coarse white fish
  (eg cod)
4 oz small mushrooms
salt and pepper

4 oz grated Sbrinz cheese
2 tablespoons butter
½ cup white wine

Butter an oblong ovenproof dish and arrange fillets in it. Season with salt and pepper. Slice mushrooms fairly thin and fry for a few minutes in butter. Cover each fillet with mushrooms and sprinkle with grated cheese. Add wine to butter in pan and heat for one minute, then pour round fish. Bake in fairly slow oven (325 deg F or No 4) for 25 to 30 minutes or until fish is cooked.

Serve with plain boiled potatoes sprinkled with finely chopped parsley. To serve 4.

FISH ROLLS IN WINE
(FISCHROLLCHEN IN WEIN)

4 large fillets of red perch
6 oz streaky bacon
2 medium onions
1 large pickled cucumber
2 teaspoons French mustard

½ cup white wine
breadcrumbs
curry powder
chopped parsley
salt and pepper

Wash and dry fillets and cut in halves lengthwise. Chop bacon and fry for a few minutes, then add chopped onion and fry until clear. Add chopped cucumber and mustard and spread this mixture on fish slices. Roll up each slice and fasten securely with wooden picks or tie with white thread. Place in buttered ovenproof dish.

Mix breadcrumbs with curry powder to taste, and sprinkle over fish rolls. Pour wine round the rolls, and bake in moderate oven (350 deg F or No 5) for 25–30 minutes. Sprinkle with chopped parsley and serve at once.

COLD SALMON TROUT WITH GREEN MAYONNAISE
(SAUMON TRUITE FROID À LA MAYONNAISE VERTE)

The first time I tasted this delectable dish was at Vevey, on the shores of the lake of Geneva or Lac Léman, as it is called in Switzerland. The lake was blue as the sky, the gardens round the lake-shore were at their best and we ate lunch outdoors watching the yachts and the steamers on the lake. It was a perfect setting for a perfect meal – a meal which is within the reach of most housewives, as even if salmon trout is not available, other whole fish can be prepared in the same way.

1 *pint white wine*		2 *lb salmon trout*
1 *pint water*		*sliced cucumber*
bouquet garni	for	*sliced lemon*
1 *sliced onion*	court	*hard-boiled egg*
1 *sliced carrot*	bouillon	*sliced tomatoes*
salt and pepper		*lettuce*
2 *whole cloves*		

Put wine and water, onion, carrot, bouquet garni, cloves, salt and pepper into a saucepan large enough to accommodate the fish, cover and simmer for 45 minutes.

Strain and return to pan. Wipe the salmon trout and remove the eyes. Tie the fish in butter muslin to enable it to be lifted easily, and lower into the court bouillon. Simmer very gently for 25 to 30 minutes (depending on size of fish), but be careful not to overcook. Allow fish to cool in bouillon, then carefully lift out and place on a serving dish big enough to hold fish and garnishings. Very carefully remove skin, leaving the head and tail intact. Place small lettuce leaves all round the fish, placing slices of tomato and hard-boiled egg in each. Arrange alternate slices of cucumber and lemon down the length of the fish, and make an 'eye' with a sprig of parsley. Serve with green mayonnaise.

GREEN MAYONNAISE
(MAYONNAISE VERTE)

1 *egg yolk*
½ *teaspoon salt*
¼ *teaspoon white pepper*
1 *tablespoon wine vinegar or lemon juice*

½ *pint olive oil*
1 *teaspoon chopped parsley*
1 *teaspoon chopped chives*
1–2 *drops green vegetable colouring*

Lightly beat the egg yolk with the salt, pepper and vinegar, using a deep bowl. Add half the olive oil, drop by drop, beating continually, then add remainder by spoonfuls, still beating until sauce is thick and all the oil is used. Add parsley and chives and, if you want a really green sauce, green colouring.

This is much simpler if you have an electric beater, or a friend to help add the olive oil as you beat the mixture.

BONDELLES
IN SAUCE NEUCHÂTELOISE

Bondelles are delicious fish found in the Lake of Neuchâtel, but any fish suitable for poaching may be used. The lake is also famous for its salmon trout, which may be cooked in the same manner as the bondelles, and served either hot or cold, with sauce Neuchâteloise or mayonnaise to which a little whipped cream has been added.

The fish are cleaned, scaled and washed. A court bouillon is made with half white wine of Neuchâtel and half water, a bouquet garni and a little salt, and the fish is poached for 10 to 15 minutes (depending on size), then lifted out and kept hot while the sauce is made. Strain the liquid in which the fish was poached.

Make the sauce by melting 1 oz butter in a small pan and blend in 1 oz flour. Slowly stir in ¾ pint strained fish stock, stirring over low heat until smooth and thickened. To this add some very small boiled onions, ½ teaspoon French mustard, ½ cup Neuchâtel white wine and a little lemon juice.

Serve with plain boiled potatoes.

SALMON, BASLE STYLE

The old Rhine town of Basle is famed for its high culinary standards, and has many local specialities, not least of which is a good supply of Rhine salmon. This is a favourite way of cooking it.

6 *slices fresh salmon*	2 *onions, chopped*
salt and pepper	3 *tablespoons stock or water*
4 *tablespoons flour*	*paprika or chopped parsley*
4 *oz butter*	

Wipe the salmon carefully but do not wash. Combine salt, pepper and flour and rub into fish all over. Melt half the butter in a frying pan and fry salmon 6 to 8 minutes on each side, until cooked through and golden brown. Remove from pan, place on heated serving dish and keep hot.

Melt remaining butter in same pan and sauté the onions over low heat for 10–15 minutes, stirring frequently, until they are soft and yellow, but do not allow to brown. Pour onions over fish. Heat stock or water in pan, scraping up any glaze remaining in pan, boiling for a minute, then pour over fish. Sprinkle with a little paprika or chopped parsley. Serve with slices of lemon and plain boiled potatoes.

PICKLED SALMON

When the supply of Rhine salmon is plentiful, housewives prepare it like this to serve in the days ahead.

Allow 1 slice of salmon cut about 1-inch thick for each portion

slices of salmon	1 *bay leaf*
good quality olive oil	1 *sprig fresh tarragon*
white wine vinegar	*piece of lemon peel*

Brush each slice of salmon on all sides with olive oil and fry until golden brown on both sides, but be very careful the fish slices do not break. Drain well and when cold put fish into a deep earthenware or glass dish with a close-fitting cover.

Boil vinegar with herbs and peel, then allow to cool. Strain over the salmon, being sure each slice is completely covered with the vinegar mixture. Pour a thin layer of olive oil over the top, cover well and store in a cold place. This will keep for at least a week.

SHRIMP AND CHEESE RAMEKINS

Delicious for supper in front of the fire on a winter's evening are these tasty shrimp ramekins, or they can be served as the first course for dinner. Either freshly cooked or frozen shrimps can be used.

4 hard-boiled eggs
½ oz butter
½ oz flour
½ pint milk
4 oz grated cheese

2 or 3 oz prepared shrimps
2 teaspoons chopped parsley
pinch cayenne
salt to taste

Melt butter in a small pan, blend in the flour, then stir in milk, stirring until mixture is smooth and thick. Cook for 2 or 3 minutes. Shell eggs and chop them roughly. Add to the sauce with the prepared shrimps, parsley, and 2 oz grated cheese. Stir occasionally until mixture is heated through and cheese is melted, but do not allow to boil. Season to taste, and divide between buttered ramekin dishes or scallop shells. Sprinkle with remainder of grated cheese and put under hot grill to lightly brown the cheese. Serve at once, with fingers of crisp toast.

EELS TICINO
(ANGUILLA ALLA TICINO)

The lakes of the Ticino region abound in many kinds of delicious-eating fish, and eels are also plentiful and used in a variety of ways. This recipe owes its inspiration to the Italian cuisine.

1½ lb eel	butter
1 gill white wine	little olive oil
1 bay leaf	1 egg
few sprigs thyme	breadcrumbs
pinch mixed spice	salt and pepper

Clean and skin eels and cut into 1-inch pieces. Place in an earthenware or ovenproof glass casserole. Mix wine, spices, herbs, salt and pepper and pour over eels, cover and cook in a moderate oven for 45 minutes. Carefully remove eels from sauce and drain well, dip in melted butter then in lightly beaten egg and coat with breadcrumbs. Fry until golden brown in butter to which a little oil has been added.

Serve with spaetzli (page 147) or buttered noodles.

EEL SOUP

This is really two dishes, as it can be served first as a soup, then the pieces of eel served as a separate course with spaghetti or spaetzli.

2 lb eel
4 medium-size potatoes
6 tomatoes
1 teaspoon lemon juice
salt and pepper
butter or oil

2 onions
1 clove of garlic (optional)
1 small bay leaf
few sprigs parsley
1 sprig thyme
4 pints water

Cut eel into 4-inch lengths, place in earthenware bowl and cover with salt, leaving overnight. Then wash well in fresh water, remove the skin, and brown the pieces in a little hot butter and oil in a deep saucepan for about 10 minutes. Peel and chop the potatoes and tomatoes and add to saucepan with the herbs, crushed garlic and seasonings to taste. Add water, bring to boil and allow to simmer for 1 hour. Add lemon juice and cook another 5 minutes.

If eels are being served separately, remove them with a slotted spoon, then sieve the soup and re-heat before serving. Or the eel pieces can be boned and returned to the soup as a substantial meal in one dish, as the country people serve it.

CHEESE DISHES

FONDUE

Fondue is the best known of Swiss dishes, and it has quite a number of variations, depending on what part of the country you are eating it in. That made in Neuchâtel is probably the best known, but if you order a fondue in Geneva you will probably get one made with the addition of eggs and butter, while in Fribourg your fondue will be made without kirsch – a sad lack, in my opinion. Usually a mixture of Gruyère and Emmental cheese is used, but all Gruyère is quite acceptable.

To make a fondue properly you must have a large, flat-bottomed earthenware dish which stands over a small spirit stove to be brought to the table. The fondue is first cooked on the kitchen stove, then put over the burner to serve at table. Each person should also be equipped with a fairly long-handled fork and a supply of one-inch bread cubes. The idea is that each person dips a piece of bread into the fondue, being careful not to lose it in the dish – if he does, he buys drinks all round. It is also considered bad manners to spill the fondue on the tablecloth, so the best way is to spear the bread, dip it in the pot and quickly swirl it round to catch the drips – and also to cool it off a little. The effort is well worth it, as fondue is not only delicious but a lot of fun.

For four persons you need:

1½ *lb mixed Gruyère and Emmental cheese*	1 *tablespoon kirsch*
4 *wine-glasses Neuchâtel white wine*	2 *cloves garlic*
1 *teaspoon potato flour or cornflour*	*pinch ground nutmeg* *pepper to taste*

Rub round the inside of the dish with a cut clove of garlic. Warm the wine in the dish over low heat, then stir in the grated cheese, stirring until cheese has melted and blended with the wine. Add remaining garlic crushed or chopped very small, nutmeg and pepper, and bring to boil. Blend cornflour with kirsch and stir into mixture, stirring all the time. In 3–4 minutes it should have thickened and can be brought to the table to keep hot over spirit lamp. It must be eaten while simmering.

Serve a Neuchâtel dry white wine with the fondue.

RACLETTE

This is another typical Swiss dish, originally from the Canton Valais, but obtainable in most parts of the country. Ideally it is made in front of the fire or a special charcoal grill, and it must be eaten with potatoes boiled in their jackets and big white pickled onions, while a bottle of white Valais wine is a fitting accompaniment. In Valais a round of cheese from either Conches or Bagnes is used, as they are quick-melting cheese, but any creamy cheese could be used. I have even seen an electric radiator pressed into service to make raclette.

The cheese is cut in two and the inner surface held to the fire until the cheese melts. The melted surface is quickly scraped off with a spatula on to a warmed plate, and you eat the rich melted cheese with the potatoes and onions. This melting, scraping and eating goes on until either the cheese is finished or your appetite is satisfied – usually the latter comes first.

CHEESE AND WINE CASSEROLE

Lausanne is a charming city, and certainly one of the easiest in the world to get lost in, with its old part of the city on different levels and no rhyme or reason to the streets. But all this confusion only adds to its charm, just as do the market stalls which are set up in the narrow, hilly streets in front of the fashionable shops – the jewel-colours of tomatoes and cucumbers vying with the elaborate and expensive jewellery displayed in the windows overlooking the vegetable stalls.

There are some excellent cooks in Lausanne, and this rich and delicious recipe was served to me by my Valais-born hostess, in an apartment high in the hills overlooking the lake. Follow her example and serve it for a special luncheon, accompanied by a salad of tomato slices set on lettuce leaves, and sprinkled with chopped chives for extra colour.

½ lb grated Gruyère cheese
1½ cups dry white wine
6 slices day-old bread
3 tablespoons butter
1 clove of garlic (optional)
6 eggs

salt and pepper
½ cup cream
½ cup chicken bouillon
¼ teaspoon dry mustard
paprika

Trim crusts from bread. Crush garlic and blend with butter, then spread bread slices. Arrange bread in buttered casserole, butter-side down. Beat eggs until foamy, season to taste, then beat in cream. Add grated cheese, wine, bouillon, mustard and paprika, stirring only enough to mix ingredients. Pour over bread. Bake in moderate oven (350 deg F or No 5) about 30 minutes, or until set and golden brown on top. Serve at once.

SCHWYZ CHEESE PIE
(SCHWYZER KÄSEKUCHEN)

This makes a rich and very tasty meatless dish.

8 oz self-raising flour
½ teaspoon salt
3 oz butter
about ¼ pint milk
4 medium-size boiled potatoes
2 eggs

8 oz grated Schwyz cheese
8 oz grated Emmental cheese
1 cup cream
2 medium onions, chopped
1 tablespoon butter (extra)

Sieve flour and salt into a basin and rub in the butter. Make a well in the centre and add milk, stirring to make a light spongy dough as for scones. Turn on to a lightly floured board, knead lightly and shape into a large round, about ½-inch thick. Carefully place on an oven slide.

Mash the potatoes until smooth, then beat in eggs and cream. Cook the onion until transparent in the extra butter and add to potatoes, then mix in the cheese. Spread this mixture evenly over the scone dough, leaving a slight margin all round, and bake in a hot oven (425 deg F or No 8).

GRUYÈRE CHEESE PIE

A rich, creamy dish which is equally good eaten hot or cold.

6 *eggs*	*salt*
6 *oz Gruyère cheese*	8 *oz flour*
4 *oz butter*	*extra grated cheese*
¾ *pint milk*	

Melt butter in a thick saucepan, add half the milk and bring to the boil. Make a smooth paste with the flour and remainder of milk and add to boiling milk, stirring all the time. Add the eggs one at a time, stirring well, then add 6 oz cheese cut into small pieces, stirring until melted. The mixture should be smooth and creamy. Pour this mixture into a deep, buttered pie dish, sprinkle with grated cheese and bake in a fairly hot oven (375 deg F or No 6) for 30 minutes.

CRÊPES DU PAYS D'ENHAUT

This is a delicious recipe suitable for a special luncheon or supper party, and the crêpes or pancakes can be made some time earlier and heated just before serving. The dish is a speciality of the Chateau d'Oex district, and was first made for me by Chef Louis Favez in one of my favourite Swiss holiday places, Châlet Bon Accueil, in this lovely district. He also introduced me to my first raclette – one of the most delectable of Swiss specialities (*see* page 63).

3 *eggs*	1 *pint milk*
8 *oz flour*	*butter and oil*
salt and pepper	*grated Gruyère cheese*
pinch ground nutmeg	*cream*

Beat the eggs, then gradually stir in the flour, salt and pepper and nutmeg to taste. Slowly stir in the milk, adding just enough to make a smooth cream. Mix oil and melted butter and use to grease a small thick pan, pouring off any surplus. Cover the bottom of the pan with a thin layer of batter, and cook until it draws away from the sides of the pan, and the top is slightly dry and set. Remove from pan without turning. As each pancake is removed from pan, sprinkle the top thickly with grated cheese and roll up at once, cheese inside. Repeat until all the mixture is used. Place the rolled pancakes in an ovenproof dish, side by side, then pour cream over the top. Sprinkle remaining cheese over the top and bake in a hot oven for 10 minutes. To serve 4.

EMMENTALER SOUFFLÉ

Emmental is a peaceful region of undulating, well-kept farmland, the big farmhouses distinctive with Bernese timber roofs and enormous eaves reaching out to their neighbours. In the summer window boxes right across the houses are ablaze with red geraniums, as if to welcome the traveller.

This district is famous for its Emmental cheese, which is easily recognized by its large holes and unmistakable fragrant aroma. It is excellent for cooking, as well as for including on the cheese tray, and this is a typical recipe from this region.

3½ oz Emmental cheese
½ lb white bread
2 tablespoons butter
2½ level tablespoons flour
1 tablespoon chopped chives

4 eggs, separated
salt, cayenne and nutmeg
1 pint milk, or half milk,
  half cream

Remove crusts from bread and cut bread into small cubes. Melt butter and fry bread cubes until a golden brown on all sides. Place in a buttered soufflé dish or casserole. Blend flour and milk and cook over low heat, stirring all the time until thickened. Allow to cool, then mix in grated cheese, beaten egg yolks, chives and seasonings. Beat egg whites until stiff and fold into cheese mixture, then pour over the bread-cubes. Put into a fairly moderate oven (No 4 or 325 deg F) and bake for 30 to 40 minutes.

APPENZELL FRITTERS
(APPENZELLER CHÄSAPPE)

These are like crisp golden fritters made in fancy patterns, something like a snail-shell pattern formed flat, if you can imagine that. They are served very hot with a vegetable or salad for a light meal, or are eaten as a snack with a glass of beer, and are a great favourite in the Appenzell region.

6 oz Appenzell cheese   ½ teaspoon baking powder
4 eggs   3–4 dessertspoons flour
1 cup milk   oil for frying
7–8 oz beer

Heat the milk and add grated cheese, stirring until melted, then cool slightly. Blend beer into flour, add baking powder, beat in eggs one at a time, then add milk and cheese mixture, beating well. If the batter is too thin add a little more flour. Heat the oil in a deep pan until very hot. Fill an icing bag with batter and quickly press through into the oil, making whirls or snail patterns of batter. Fry quickly until golden brown, lift out with a slotted spoon on to a hot plate and serve at once.

CHEESE AND MUSHROOM PIE

Whenever I make this pie for my family it brings back memories of one of the most enjoyable and unforgettable picnics I have ever had. We had travelled by the rack and pinion train from Zermatt, a 5,000 foot climb through snowfields and magnificent scenery to

Gornergrat, and nearly the whole fifty minutes climb was in view of the Matterhorn, surely the most wonderful mountain of them all. Although there is a hotel with a good restaurant at Gornergrat, we had taken a picnic lunch with us from Zermatt, and included were two of these cheese and mushroom pies, enough to feed at least four instead of the two of us. But the mountain air gave us appetite, and we ate every last crumb and found them delicious. They are also excellent served hot.

1 *lb short pastry*	$\frac{1}{2}$ *oz plain flour*
6 *oz mushrooms*	$\frac{1}{4}$ *pint milk*
1$\frac{1}{2}$ *oz butter or margarine*	*salt and pepper to taste*
3 *oz grated cheese*	1 *egg*

Turn out the pastry on a lightly floured board and roll out thinly into a large square, about 12 by 12 inches. Trim the edges neatly with a sharp knife. Have the oven heated to 425 deg F or No 8, and grease an oven tray.

Slice the mushrooms and cook them in 1 oz of butter for 3 or 4 minutes, turning frequently. While they are cooking make the sauce by melting the remainder of the butter in a small pan, then blend in flour and cook over low heat for 2 minutes, stirring all the time. Remove from heat and stir in milk and seasonings and the juices from the mushrooms, stirring well until blended. Return to low heat and keep stirring until mixture boils and thickens. Continue cooking gently, still stirring, for about 3 minutes, then stir in cheese until it is melted. Add mushrooms, and put sauce aside to cool.

When cool, put the mushroom mixture into the middle of the pastry square, spreading over the centre part only. Brush edges of pastry with beaten egg and carefully fold each corner into the centre, rather like making a square envelope. Pinch edges together to make a ½-inch seal on each join. Brush over top of pie with beaten egg and carefully slide on to greased oven tray. Bake in hot oven for 30 to 40 minutes until golden brown.

Various other ingredients can be added to the cheese sauce as desired, such as asparagus, chopped ham, cooked fish, or chopped salami sausage.

CHEESE TARTS
(RAMEQUINS DE FROMAGE)

These are excellent for a party supper, they can be served with salad for lunch or left in their tins and packed for a picnic meal. If preferred the same recipe can be made up into one large tart.

½ lb Gruyère cheese, grated	pinch dry mustard
¼ cup grated onion	pinch cayenne
2 dessertspoons butter	salt and pepper
3 eggs	short pastry
1½ cups light cream	

Roll pastry ⅛-inch thick and line 12 3-inch tart shells. Sauté onion in butter for 5 minutes. Add to grated cheese and toss lightly to mix well. Beat eggs well, then beat in cream, seasonings, and cheese-onion mixture, blending lightly. Divide between the lined tart shells. Bake in a fairly hot oven (400 deg F or No 7) for 20 minutes or until custard is set and golden brown and pastry cooked. Serve hot or cold.

TRIANGLES DE GRUYÈRE

Petits Gruyères are those foil-wrapped triangles of
cheese which are so useful for cooking. Cut required
number of triangles into two, leaving the foil on while
you cut with a sharp knife. Roll short pastry out ½-inch
thick and cut into triangles a little larger than the
cheese. Sandwich a slice of cheese between two triangles
of pastry, adding a sprinkle of chives to the cheese.
Seal edges of pastry firmly, brush over tops with milk
and bake in hot oven (425 deg F or No 8) for about
15 minutes, or until pastry is golden brown. Serve hot
or cold.

ONION RAREBIT

These were served to me for supper one Autumn evening in Berne, when my hostess told me of the historic
onion market which is held annually in October in the
capital city. Some weeks later I visited the market to
see it for myself, and certainly found it a fascinating
sight, although a little odoriferous, with great strings
of onions hanging from numerous stalls erected in the
market place—right opposite the Swiss Houses of Parliament. Housewives come from all the surrounding
districts to the Berne onion market to buy the winter's
supply of this very important commodity, and then at
night there are various celebrations in the streets.

This recipe is certainly a delicious way of using up
some of the onions bought at the market. Allow one
rarebit for each serve.

6 *rather thick slices of bread*	*butter or margarine*
6 *thick slices Gruyère cheese*	*paprika*
4 *large onions*	

Slice onions very fine and pour boiling water over them, allowing to stand for 5 minutes, then drain well. Fry the bread until golden on both sides, drain well and place on a baking sheet. In the same pan as used for frying bread, fry the onions until pale golden, but do not allow them to get too dark. Spread the onions over the fried bread slices, cover each with a slice of Gruyère, top with a small pat of butter and a dusting of paprika. Bake in a hot oven or under the griller until cheese has melted. Serve at once.

CHEESE FRITTERS
(ESCALOPES AU FROMAGE)

10 oz *Tilsit cheese*   *French mustard*
1 *large egg*   *paprika*
fine browned breadcrumbs   *butter or oil*

Cut cheese in 4 thick slices, all the same size. Spread lightly with mustard and sprinkle with paprika. Pass through beaten egg then coat with breadcrumbs, repeating this operation. Heat butter or oil in large thick pan and fry slices quickly until golden, turning to brown both sides. Serve at once, garnished with parsley.

RAMEQUIN VAUDOIS

8 *slices bread*   ¾ *pint milk*
8 *slices cheese*   *salt, pepper and pinch dry*
2 *eggs*   *mustard*

Butter an oblong casserole and arrange two rows of alternate slices of bread and cheese. Beat the eggs with the seasonings, add milk and pour over the bread and cheese. Stand for 10 minutes, then place casserole in a dish of water and bake in a moderate oven (350 deg F or No 5) for 30 minutes, or until set.

CHEESE SNACKS FROM BERNE
(CROÛTES BERNOISES)

12 *slices bread*   ⅛ *pint milk*
butter   1 *tablespoon kirsch*
¾ *lb grated Emmental cheese*   *paprika*
4 *eggs, separated*

Beat egg yolks with milk, add cheese and kirsch, then
fold in well-beaten egg whites. Dip bread slices in this
mixture. Melt butter in large frying pan and when
frothy gently place bread slices in pan and fry until
crisp and golden, turning to brown on both sides.
Sprinkle with a little paprika and serve at once.

CHEESE SNACKS FROM BASLE
(CROÛTES BÂLOISES)

6 *slices bread*   *butter*
4 *onions*   *paprika*
6 *slices Gruyère cheese*

The slices of cheese should be nearly the same size as
the bread slices. Slice onions very thin and fry until
golden in butter. Toast the bread and butter lightly,
keep hot. Put aside 2 tablespoons fried onions and
spread remainder evenly over the hot toast. Place a slice
of cheese on each slice of toast and put under hot griller
just long enough to melt the cheese. Garnish with
remainder of fried onions and sprinkle with paprika.
Serve at once.

NOODLES WITH GRUYÈRE
(GRATIN GRUYÈRIEN AUX NOUILLES)

1 *lb noodles*	1½ *cups milk*
6 *oz Gruyère cheese, grated*	1 *cup water*
3 *eggs, separated*	*salt and pepper*
2 *dessertspoons flour*	2 *cups chopped, cooked ham*

Cook noodles in boiling, salted water for 5 minutes or until tender. Melt butter in saucepan and blend in flour, cook for a minute, then slowly stir in milk and water, stirring until thickened and smooth. Cook for 3 minutes, stirring at intervals. Add cheese and stir until melted, then remove from heat. Beat egg yolks in a basin until well mixed, then add 2 spoonfuls of cheese sauce, mix well and add egg mixture to sauce. Return to stove over low heat and stir until heated, but be careful not to let it boil. Season to taste then fold in well-beaten egg whites. Mix noodles and ham in buttered casserole and pour sauce over them. Bake in moderate oven (350 deg F or No 5) for 20–30 minutes. Serve at once.

PILATUS CHEESE PIE
(TARTE DE FROMAGE PILATUS)

Pilatus is the snow-capped mountain overlooking the very charming and picturesque city of Lucerne, and this tasty pie with its meringue topping resembling snow is a speciality of a little restaurant in that city. Incidentally, if you visit Lucerne, do not fail to travel up Pilatus by aerial cableway, returning down the other side by a spectacular rack and pinion railway, one of the most thrilling rides you could experience. But back to our pie . . .

8 oz short pastry
1 oz butter or margarine
1 oz flour
½ pint milk
6 oz grated cheese

2 eggs, separated
salt and pepper
pinch cayenne
1 oz grated Parmesan cheese
rice or breadcrusts

Roll out pastry and line an 8-inch pie-plate or sandwich tin. Prick base lightly with a fork, line with a piece of greaseproof paper and fill with rice or crusts to prevent pastry rising as it bakes. Bake in hot oven (400 deg F or No 6) for 20 minutes, then remove paper and crusts or rice and continue baking for a few minutes to cook centre. Remove from oven when pale golden and crisp.

Make filling by melting butter in saucepan over low heat, then blend in flour and cook for a minute. Remove from heat and slowly stir in milk, then return to stove and bring to boil, stirring continually. Remove from heat and stir in cheese, lightly beaten egg yolks and seasonings. Pour into baked pastry case. Beat egg whites with a pinch of salt until stiff enough to stand in peaks. Spread roughly over the cheese filling, bringing to a slight peak in the centre (like a mountain), then sprinkle with the Parmesan cheese. Bake in moderately hot oven for about 10 minutes until meringue is firm and set.

This should serve 4 to 6, either hot as a savoury course, or cold with salad.

VEAL AND EGG ROLLS
(KALBSSCHNITZEL NACH JOSCA)

Veal is probably the most popular meat in Switzerland, and it is always of a very high quality, although usually rather younger than we are accustomed to. There are many variations of these veal rolls (a version of our veal birds) with different fillings, used in different parts of the country (*see* Bocconcini). This version comes from Wildhaus, in the Obertoggenburg Valley, a delightful spot for either a summer or winter holiday.

6 *thin veal cutlets*	2 *carrots, sliced*
6 *hard-boiled eggs*	1 *bay leaf*
1 *sliced onion*	*fat*
salt and pepper	*flour*

The cutlets should be pounded fairly thin without breaking. Roll each cutlet round a shelled egg, season with salt and pepper, and tie firmly with thread. Melt fat in saucepan and brown veal rolls on all sides, then add onion and brown slightly. Add enough water or stock just to cover rolls, add carrot and bay leaf and simmer gently for 35–40 minutes, or until veal is cooked. Remove rolls to a heated serving dish, cut off thread, and keep hot. Strain sauce in pan and thicken with a little blended flour, then pour over rolls. Serve with noodles or spaetzli (page 155).

ESCALOPES LOCARNO

Tender enough to cut with a fork, and attractive enough to make a picture on the plate before I started to eat, these veal escalopes were served to me in sun-bathed Locarno, on Lake Maggiore, in the Italian part of Switzerland.

Locarno, set beside the lovely lake, is ideal for a holiday, and makes a good base for excursions into the delightful valleys behind it, travelling either by train or postal bus.

These escalopes are easy to prepare and make a tasty change from the usual veal cutlets. Buy young veal slices and ask the butcher to flatten them for you, or do it yourself with a meat mallet or back of a thick wooden spoon. Be careful not to break the slices.

In addition to the required number of escalopes you need a slice of Gruyère cheese and two or three anchovy fillets for each escalope, flour, salt and pepper, butter and a little olive oil.

Toss each escalope in flour seasoned with salt and pepper. Melt some butter in a thick pan and add a little olive oil, and when hot brown the veal quickly on both sides. It should be cooked – but not overcooked, or it will be dry. When golden on both sides, place a slice of cheese on top of each escalope, then arrange anchovy fillets on top of cheese. Put under a hot griller just long enough to melt the cheese, and serve immediately.

BOCCONCINI

This is another Italian-inspired dish which I first tasted in Ascona. For each person you need 2 or 3 thin slices of young veal, the same number of slices of cooked ham cut the same size as the veal, a finger of Gruyère cheese for each slice of veal. Also salt and pepper, butter and ½ cup white wine.

Pound the veal until the slices are as thin as possible without breaking. On each slice of veal place a slice of ham, then a finger of cheese, roll up firmly and fasten with wooden toothpicks or tie with thread. Season to taste. Melt the butter in a thick pan and gently brown the veal rolls on all sides. Add the wine (or tomato purée may be added here instead of wine if preferred) cook for a minute, then cover and cook for about 10 minutes until veal is tender. Serve at once, with the juices in the pan poured over the veal rolls.

VEAL STEAK FORESTIÈRE

2 lbs veal steak (½-inch thick)   1 clove of garlic
1 tablespoon lemon juice   3 oz butter
salt and pepper   6 oz button mushrooms

Cut veal into cubes and toss in lemon juice, season with salt and pepper and stand for a few minutes. Melt 2 oz butter in thick pan, add garlic and veal. Cook veal until lightly browned, turning at intervals to brown evenly on all sides. Remove from pan and keep hot. Melt remaining butter in pan and add cleaned mushrooms, cooking for 10 minutes with cover on pan, and turning at intervals. Remove garlic, pour mushrooms and juices in pan over veal and serve at once.

This is good served with spaetzli (page 155).

VEAL GRUYÈRE

Prepare as above, but add cooked veal to pan with mushrooms when they are cooked. Cover with thin slices Gruyère cheese and put under hot griller for 2–3 minutes, or just long enough for cheese to melt. Serve at once.

CHOPPED VEAL
(EMINCÉ DE VEAU)

This is a very popular dish all over Switzerland, many places having their own version of the same dish. The meat is not minced but is cut, either by hand or by a special machine, into tiny squares about ¼-inch thick.

For each serve allow 4 oz thinly cut veal steak, 1 small onion, 1 oz butter, flour, salt and pepper.

Chop the meat as directed above, sprinkle with flour, salt and pepper. Chop the onion small and sauté in butter until tender but not browned. Add the meat and cook quickly over good heat for 2–3 minutes. The meat being in such small pieces should cook in that time. Add a squeeze of lemon juice and serve with risotto or *rösti*.

In Zürich I have eaten this dish made as above with the addition of chopped mushrooms (Emincé de Veau à la Zurichoise) and in St Gall a little cream was poured over the cooked meat and onions at the last minute. All three ways were good, so take your choice.

OSSO BUCO

This is the Swiss version of the popular Italian dish of the same name (or it is sometimes spelled Osso Bucchi), and it is a favourite in the Tessin district.

It is made with shin or knuckle of young veal, and you should ask the butcher to saw it into 2-inch pieces (saw, not chop, as the marrow should remain inside the bone).

2 *lb shin or knuckle of veal*
1 *clove of garlic, chopped*
3 *onions, sliced*
2 *leeks, sliced*
2 *stalks of celery, chopped*
3 *oz butter*
salt and pepper

2 *cups stock*
¼ *pint white wine*
¾ *lb peeled, chopped tomatoes*
½ *oz flour*
1 *teaspoon lemon juice*
chopped parsley

Heat butter in a large pan and brown the veal on all sides, then remove. Add prepared vegetables and cook in butter in the same pan, turning as they cook, and do not brown too much. Replace meat, arranging the pieces so they remain upright in the pan to keep the marrow in place as the meat cooks. Add tomatoes, wine and flour blended with the stock and seasoning to taste. Cover and simmer for about 2 to 2½ hours, or until meat is tender. Add lemon juice just before serving, and sprinkle with chopped parsley.

This should be served with risotto or noodles.

VEAL SWEETBREADS
WITH TARRAGON
(RIS DE VEAU À LA ESTRAGON)

A delicious dish from the Neuchâtel district, where it is usually served with a glass of the excellent local wine.

2 *calves sweetbreads*	3–4 *oz butter*
flour	1 *medium onion*
salt and pepper	*chopped tarragon*
triangles of Petit Gruyère	1 *cup dry white wine*
½ *bay leaf*	2 *sprigs of parsley*

Soak sweetbreads in cold water for 1 hour, with a little salt. Put into saucepan with fresh cold water, ½ bay leaf and sprigs of parsley and bring to boil, then boil for 3 minutes. Drain sweetbreads and plunge into cold water until cool enough to handle, then remove all skin and fat and cut in slices. Dip slices into flour seasoned with salt and pepper.

Melt half the butter in a pan and cook the finely chopped onion until pale golden. Add remainder of butter and gently fry the sweetbread slices until browned on one side. Sprinkle with chopped tarragon before turning to brown on other side. When cooked cover with sliced Gruyère cheese, then pour wine over the top. Place under a moderately hot griller until cheese is melted slightly and sauce bubbles. Serve with boiled potatoes.

FRITTURA MISTA

In the Canton of the Grisons (a region of 150 or more valleys, with a list of dishes which owe their inspiration to many varying cultures) a special treat is the *frittura mista*, which consists of various foods dipped in batter and fried.

The most usual ingredients are small pieces of veal, pieces of calves' liver, brains, sweetbreads, sometimes chicken breasts, and pieces of aubergine, mushrooms or cauliflower. These are prepared, then dipped in batter and fried in very hot oil until crisp and golden brown. The little mouthfuls are then piled on a hot dish, garnished with slices of lemon and eaten at once – this last direction being very important, because like all foods fried in batter they must not be kept waiting.

Make the batter with

4 oz flour	1 teacup of slightly warmed
3 tablespoons olive oil	water
salt	1 egg white

Sieve the flour into a basin, stir in the oil until well blended, add salt and water and stir until like a smooth cream. Stand for at least 2 hours, then when batter is to be used fold in the stiffly beaten egg white. Dip foods to be fried into the batter then fry in deep, hot oil. This batter can be used for all kinds of foods, a little sugar being added for fruits.

SNAILS BÜRGERART
(SCHNECKEN NACH BÜRGERART)

In the old days the Ticino housewives fed snails on grape leaves for at least a week before cooking them, but today you can buy cleaned snails in tins, accompanied by a packet containing the cleaned shells, all ready to be prepared and cooked. If you have never eaten snails before, try this way as a special entreé or first course for dinner.

Wash the snail shells well in salted boiling water. Rinse and place upside-down to drain. Allow 6 per person.

4 oz breadcrumbs   salt and pepper
10 shelled, chopped walnuts   pinch ground nutmeg
½ cup grated cheese   butter

Blend all above ingredients together with a pestle and mortar (or use the back of a wooden spoon in a thick, shallow bowl), adding butter as necessary to make a good stiff paste. Replace snails in shells and cover with nut mixture. Place on ovenproof platter with openings upwards and bake for 5–6 minutes in moderate oven, or place under hot griller. Garnish with sprigs of parsley and serve at once.

If you have difficulty in keeping the snail shells in place, crumple a piece of aluminium cooking foil and make small depressions in it to hold the shells as they cook. They can also be served on this.

TRIPE, THURGAU STYLE

1½ lb well-cooked tripe
2 onions, sliced
1 clove of garlic, chopped
1 cup beef stock
beef dripping

1 cup dry white wine or cider
1 tablespoon flour
2 tablespoons tomato paste
salt and pepper

Lightly fry onions and garlic in dripping until golden. Cut well-washed tripe in thin strips and fry with onions until lightly browned, turning frequently. Sprinkle with flour, salt and pepper and add wine or cider with stock. Cover and simmer for 1 hour. Stir in tomato paste and cook for another 15 minutes. Serve at once, for four.

TRIPE À LA NEUCHÂTELOISE

2½ lb cooked tripe
1 calf's foot or pig's trotter
2 leeks
½ lb carrots
1 stalk of celery
2 onions, sliced

bouquet garni
2 whole cloves
1 cup white wine
1 pint water
salt and pepper

Blanche the calf's foot or trotter in boiling water and trim well. Cut tripe into pieces. Put all ingredients together into a large saucepan and bring to boil, then simmer until tripe and trotter are tender, about 3–4 hours.

To serve, the tripe is removed and kept warm, the meat is cut from the foot or trotter and added to the tripe, then the sauce in pan is strained and thickened with a roux of butter and flour and poured over tripe mixture.

PORK CHOPS GRUYÈRE

I had just returned to Montreux after a trip into the Fribourgeois Alps to visit the town of Gruyères, in the district where the famous Gruyère cheese is made. Looking at the dinner menu I saw 'Pork Chops Gruyère', and decided it was a fitting dish to end an enjoyable day. Certainly, Gruyères is a very picturesque little medieval town, perched on top of a hill, with white-fronted old houses lining the terraced streets, and it is reached through most interesting country.

My pork chop was also very interesting, and well worth your making, but I should warn you it is not a dish for dieters!

4 *pork chops (preferably cut*   *salt and pepper*
  from the fillet)   1 *teaspoon mixed mustard*
bacon fat or butter   *a little thick cream*
4 *oz Gruyère cheese, grated fine*

Blend cheese, mustard and thick cream to make a smooth paste, and let stand for a few minutes. Trim excess fat from chops, and sauté them in a thick pan in the bacon fat, turning to cook both sides. Season to taste.

When chops are cooked, spread the cheese mixture generously over one side of each chop and put under a hot grill until lightly browned. Serve at once with plain boiled potatoes.

BRAISED PIGS' TROTTERS
(RAGOÛT DE PIEDS DE PORC)

Berne, the capital of Switzerland, is a picturesque and charming city. Food is of great importance there, and the dignity of Parliament is in no way impaired by the colourful vegetable market which appears every week in the square in front of the impressive Parliament House. There are a number of interesting restaurants under the old arcades lining streets in the old part of the city, and here you can enjoy the famous Bernerplatte, a vast tasty mixture of pigs' trotters, tongue, bacon, ham and Bernese smoked sausage arranged round a mountain of sauerkraut, and served with boiled potatoes and beans. The English housewife will find the following dish of pigs' trotters not quite so complicated as the Bernerplatte, and it makes an appetising meal for a cold winter's day. You can serve it with sauerkraut (this can be bought in tins and heated) or with braised red cabbage (page 40) as I enjoyed it in Berne.

6 *small pigs' trotters*	2 *onions, sliced*
1 *large clove of garlic (optional)*	2 *carrots, diced*
salt and pepper	1 *bay leaf*
3 *whole cloves*	*flour*
pork fat	

Wash the trotters well and dry. Rub well with the cut garlic, then with salt and pepper. Heat the fat and fry trotters until browned on all sides. Add onions, carrots, bay leaf, cloves and enough boiling water to cover the meat. Cover, and simmer for $3\frac{1}{2}$ to 4 hours, or until meat is almost falling from the bones. Remove cloves and bay leaf and thicken gravy with a little flour.

FRICASSEE OF PORK
(SCHWEINS-FRIKASSEE)

This is a favourite country dish during the cold winter months.

2–3 *lb back cut of pork*	*sprigs thyme and bay leaf*
1 *cup pig's blood*	2 *tablespoons pork fat or lard*
dry red wine	1 *heaped tablespoon flour*
salt and peppercorns	*small whole onions*
2 *whole cloves*	1 *cup cream*

Dice the meat and put into a basin with seasonings and herbs and cover with wine, or a mixture of half wine and half water. Leave in a cool place for 24 hours, stirring occasionally. Drain meat and brown in hot fat, then stir in flour and brown well. Add wine marinade and simmer, covered, for 2 hours. Mix blood and cream together and stir into mixture, then re-heat without allowing to boil. Serve with boiled potatoes.

BACON AND PEAR STEW
(SCHNITZ UND MOCKE)

The dried pears give this a most distinctive and pleasant flavour.

1 *lb dried pears*	2¼ *lb potatoes, sliced thickly*
¾ *pint hot water*	*salt and pepper*
¼ *lb smoked bacon*	½ *cup cream*

Pour boiling water over pears and leave for some hours or overnight. Cut bacon into cubes and fry in a fair-size pan for 2–3 minutes, then add pears and the water in which they were soaked, cover and simmer for 30 minutes. Add potatoes, season to taste and continue cooking until potatoes are tender. Add cream and serve.

LAMB STEW
(BLANQUETTE D'AGNEAU)

This Valais dish is made with either lamb or kid, and garnished with the asparagus which is famous in the district.

1½–2 lb lamb from thick end of leg	2 oz butter
stock or water	2 egg yolks
bouquet garni (a sprig of parsley, thyme and a bay leaf tied together)	2 dessertspoons flour
	lemon juice
	2 tablespoons cream
18 small onions	6 thin slices cooked ham
salt and pepper	18 cooked asparagus spears

Cut meat into cubes, put into saucepan with bouquet garni, salt, pepper and enough stock to cover generously. Cover pan and simmer for about 1½ hours, adding peeled onions after about 45 minutes. When meat is tender, strain off liquor into a bowl and keep meat hot on serving platter over hot water. Melt the butter and stir in flour, blending well, then gradually stir in meat liquor, continually stirring until sauce is smooth and creamy. Continue cooking over low heat for 5–6 minutes, then remove from heat and stir in beaten egg yolks. Put back over low heat and stir until eggs have been absorbed, then stir in cream and finally the lemon juice. Heat, but on no account allow sauce to boil.

Pour sauce over meat and garnish platter with asparagus spears rolled in slices of ham, allowing 3 asparagus spears to each slice of ham. Serve with young peas and boiled potatoes rolled in finely chopped parsley.

In Valais the asparagus would be rolled in thin slices of home-cured jambon cru, a delicious smoked ham which is eaten uncooked, and cut in paper-thin slices.

STUFFED BEEF
(HUSARENBRATEN)

2½ lb topside steak
3 oz calf's liver
3 oz soft breadcrumbs
milk
butter
2 egg yolks
flour

1 onion, sliced
¼ lb small mushrooms
bouquet garni
1 rasher bacon, chopped
½ pint meat stock
½ cup sour cream (optional)
salt and pepper

Have the topside cut as a square piece, then ask the butcher to cut it in 1-inch slices about three-quarters of the way through the meat, like a book with thick leaves attached at the back.

Soak the liver in warm water for ten minutes, then drain and chop fairly small. Soak the breadcrumbs in a little milk, then squeeze dry and mix with liver. Melt 1½ oz butter in pan and fry the liver mixture, then cool and mix with egg yolks. Season the slices of beef with salt and pepper and spread the liver stuffing evenly between them, then tie meat firmly but not too tightly with thin string, keeping it in shape. Roll in flour and brown in butter on all sides until well browned. Add onion, bouquet garni, bacon, mushrooms and stock, cover and simmer very slowly for 2 to 2½ hours, or until meat is tender.

Remove the meat to a hot serving plate and keep hot while you make gravy. Strain off stock from pan, skim off fat, and thicken with 1 oz flour mixed with sour cream or water. Bring to boil, stirring all the time, then add mushrooms from saucepan. Serve meat cut across the slices, with the mushroom gravy, and either noodles or spaetzli (see page 155).

FONDUE BOURGUIGNONNE

This is one of those spectacular dishes which make a meal an event of great importance. Although of French inspiration, it is also very popular in Switzerland.

For those who have never partaken of it, a few words of explanation are necessary. It is essentially a meal for at least four people, who sit round a table in the middle of which is an iron or copper pot standing over a spirit lamp. The pot is full of very hot oil, and in front of each diner is a plate of steak cubes – the best cut of steak, naturally – and a two-pronged, long-handled fork. In addition there are arranged round the table a number of small dishes of appetising and piquant sauces. So much for the initial stages.

Now each person impales a steak cube firmly on a fork and plunges it into the boiling oil (be careful not to lose your steak) cooking just until meat is done to your liking. Dip your steak cube into one of the sauces – try not to drip it all over the tablecloth – and eat it very carefully, as it is sure to be hotter than you think, unless you have chosen one of the cold sauces for your dunking. The idea is to try all the sauces in turn, or you can keep to the one you fancy. Go on cooking steak cubes and dunking them until steak and sauces are used up, or you lose your appetite, whichever comes first.

I have eaten this Fondue Bourguignonne in several different countries and enjoyed it, but another version of the same dish which I enjoyed still more was one I was served in Rapperswil, on Lake of Zürich. This was at a small hotel in the picturesque old town square, the Freihof, where Frau Egli had prepared one of the most delightful meals we had ever eaten, to give us a delightful memory of Rapperswil.

FONDUE RAPPERSWIL

The basic idea of this is the same as in the preceding recipe, but instead of boiling oil, the pan over the spirit stove was full of well seasoned beef bouillon, boiling gently.

In front of each place were six small bowls, each containing a different sauce or garnish. These were Sauce Béarnaise, grated horseradish mixed with whipped cream, a well-flavoured curry sauce, soya sauce, a piquant tomato and onion sauce, and a bowl of chopped glacé fruits sprinkled with cayenne.

The steak was cut in paper thin strips, quite easy to wrap round the two-pronged forks, and cooked very quickly in the boiling bouillon.

After we had finished the steak, two egg yolks were quickly stirred into the bouillon, and it was served as a soup course, although nobody had any appetite left. I must also tell you that after all this we were served paper-thin crêpes filled with apricot conserve and flamed with rum – certainly a meal to remember.

But the Fondue Rapperswil is one you could prepare at home for a special occasion, needing only a thick pot and a spirit stove over which the bouillon boils. The sauces, however many you prefer, need not be elaborate, but they should be well flavoured, and each one different. The bouillon, which gains in richness with each piece of steak, can be served next day for dinner.

FONDUE BACCHUS

Another version of the preceding recipe, this time one I enjoyed at the Hotel Bellevue, set in the sloping vineyards up above Lausanne.

The steak was cut very thin (I was told the simplest way to cut meat almost paper-thin was to freeze it and cut it with a sharp freezer knife), then made into little rolls. The rolls are speared on forks and cooked in a mixture of beef bouillon and strong red wine, and served with a variety of sauces.

A special Fondue created for the Vevey Fête de Vignerons is made with tender young veal rolls (as in above recipe) cooked in a mixture of veal bouillon and dry white wine, accompanied by various sauces.

BEAN HOT-POT

This is a good country dish for cold winter days, made in many Alpine farmhouses where it is left to cook slowly on the old-fashioned iron range. But it is just as easily made in our modern kitchens, and is an interesting and economical dish.

1 lb white haricot beans
1 large onion, sliced
1 oz bacon fat or lard
1 clove garlic, finely chopped
2 pork sausages
2 frankfurters
2-inch piece good quality salami
1 beef stock cube
1 bay leaf
2 tablespoons brown sugar
1 teaspoon mixed mustard
2 tablespoons tomato paste
salt and pepper

Wash beans well, cover with cold water and soak over-night. Next day boil the beans in the same water in which they were soaked for about $\frac{3}{4}$ hour, until soft but not completely cooked (the time varies with different types of beans). Be careful they do not boil dry.

While beans are cooking melt fat in a pan and cook the onion and garlic until soft but not browned. Add the pork sausages and brown quickly on all sides.

When beans are nearly cooked drain them but reserve the liquor, making it up to 1 pint with water and a stock cube. Add sugar, tomato paste, bay leaf, mustard, salt and pepper, and mix well. Place beans in a deep casserole. Slice the frankfurters and sausages into chunks, cut the salami into dice (remove skin) and add to the beans with the onions and the fat in the pan. Mix in the liquid and stir well.

Cover casserole, put into a slow oven (325 deg F or No 3) and bake for about 1 hour, or until beans are soft and the stock nearly absorbed. Stir gently before serving, and sprinkle with chopped parsley. Serves 4 or 5.

MUTTON CHOPS WITH ONIONS

Another farmhouse recipe which the farmwives make as the days grow colder – and the sheep grow older and tougher.

6 *thick mutton chops*	*salt and pepper*
butter or lard	2 *cups stock*
1 *clove of garlic, chopped*	2 *lb potatoes*
1 *lb onions, sliced thin*	*chopped parsley*

Brown chops on both sides in a little fat, remove from pan and lightly brown the onions and garlic in the same pan. Place half the chops in an ovenproof casserole, cover with half the onions, then remainder of chops and finish with a layer of onions. Add the boiling stock, season to taste, cover and cook in a moderate oven (350 deg F or No 4) for 30 minutes.

Peel and slice the potatoes and arrange in the top of the casserole. Replace in oven, covered, for 20 minutes; then remove lid and cook another 20 minutes, basting with stock in casserole, and which should be almost absorbed by the time cooking is completed. Sprinkle with parsley and serve at once. Serves 6.

HAM WITH MUSHROOMS

A simple dish from the vineyard country bordering Lac Leman, but one which is delicious enough for a dinner party.

4 *thick slices cooked ham*	6 *oz button mushrooms, sliced*
1 *large onion, chopped*	½ *pint inexpensive white wine*
1 *clove of garlic, chopped*	4 *tablespoons thick cream*
2 *tablespoons butter*	*sprinkle of pepper*

Cook the onion and garlic in the butter in a deep covered pan until soft. Add the mushrooms, then cover with slices of ham and pour over the wine. Cover and simmer over gentle heat until the ham is heated through and the mushrooms cooked. Remove the ham and keep hot.

Boil up the pan to reduce liquid slightly, then stir in cream and heat without allowing to boil. Pour over the ham and serve at once.

LAMB AND VEGETABLE STEW

A dish I enjoyed in a little village inn near St Gallen.

2 lbs shoulder of lamb
oil
salt and pepper
thyme
1 clove garlic, chopped
2 medium onions, sliced

1 lb potatoes, peeled
3–4 carrots, sliced
4 sticks celery, sliced
¼ pint white wine or cider
½ pint stock

Rub the meat over well with salt and pepper, thyme and garlic, then brown in a little oil with the onions in a deep ovenproof casserole. Cover and cook in a moderate oven (350 deg F or No 4) for 45 minutes.

Place prepared vegetables round the meat, add wine or cider and stock, cover and continue cooking for 1 hour more.

When meat is tender cut in slices and serve with vegetables from casserole. Serves 4.

HEAVEN AND EARTH

This is a recipe from the German part of Switzerland and gets its name from the combination of potatoes (earth) and apples (heaven).

1½ lb potatoes, peeled
1 lb cooking apples
2 tablespoons sugar
2 medium onions, chopped

2 or 3 rashers bacon, diced
bacon fat or lard
salt and pepper
1 large black pudding

Cook potatoes until soft in salted water. Peel, quarter and core apples and cook with sugar until soft. Mash the potatoes, mix in apples and beat together until smooth. Fry bacon until crisp, remove from pan and fry onion until golden. Drain well and add to potato and apple mixture, season to taste with salt and pepper.

Cut black pudding in halves lengthwise and cross-wise. Fry in bacon fat until skin curls away.

Heap potato and apple mixture on four plates and top with pieces of black pudding. To serve 4.

If preferred, slices of fried liver can be substituted for the black pudding.

OX-TONGUE WITH CAPER SAUCE

Basle, on the borders where France and Germany meet, is a picturesque old city where you will find some good restaurants serving food inspired by the cuisine of both the neighbouring countries. This is from the German side.

1 *ox-tongue*   2 *carrots*
2 *sticks celery*   ½ *oz seeded raisins*
1 *parsnip*   *wineglass of Madeira or*
1 *large onion*   *wine vinegar*
1 *clove garlic*   1 *tablespoon capers*

Soak the tongue overnight. Next day put into a large saucepan with enough water to cover. Add cleaned and chopped vegetables, wine or vinegar and raisins. Bring to the boil, then simmer, covered tightly, for 3 hours or until tender.

Remove tongue from pan, draining well, but retain the stock. Remove the skin and gristle at base of the tongue, also small bones. Cut tongue in thick slices.

Make a sauce by rubbing the vegetables from the stock through a sieve. Return this purée to the stock, thicken with a little blended cornflour and boil until thick and smooth. Add capers and taste for seasoning, then replace tongue in sauce to re-heat.

Instead of capers, sliced mushrooms may be cooked in the sauce before thickening.

PORK CHOPS WITH SOUR CREAM

4 pork chops
butter
salt and pepper

$\frac{1}{4}$ pint sour cream
flour
capers

Trim chops of any excess fat and rub over with salt and pepper. Melt butter in a thick pan and brown chops on both sides for about 5 minutes each. Add cream and simmer gently for another 20 minutes, turning chops half way through cooking time, until they are tender. Remove chops from pan and keep hot. Blend a little flour into sauce in the pan to thicken and add capers, pour over chops and serve with noodles.

LIVER LOAF

This can be served either hot or cold, and carries well for a picnic.

1½ *lb ox liver, sliced*
½ *lb fat bacon, chopped*
1 *onion, chopped*
2 *white bread rolls*

little milk
salt and pepper
pinch marjoram or thyme
½ *lb short pastry*

Soak rolls in milk and squeeze dry. Soak liver in cold water, drain well and remove tubes. Put twice through the mincer with onion and bacon, then mix in bread, salt and pepper and herbs, blending well. Line a loaf tin with the pastry, then fill with liver mixture, levelling off the top. Bake in a moderate oven (350 deg F or No 5) for one hour. Turn out and cut in slices.

KIDNEY RAGOUT

The Valais produces an abundance of wine, both red and white, and the housewives season many of their favourite dishes with wine. This is one I tasted in that area which I find very useful at home.

1 *lb ox kidney*
4 *tablespoons butter*
1 *medium onion, chopped*
4 *tablespoons flour*
¾ *pint beef stock*
sprig fresh thyme

4 *tablespoons dry red wine*
4 *tablespoons tomato paste*
salt and pepper
chopped parsley
noodles

Soak kidney in cold water with a little vinegar for 1 hour. Drain well, cut in halves lengthwise and remove hard white core. Cut in slices.

Melt butter in a thick pan and cook the onions for 5 minutes. Add kidneys and sauté with onions until cooked through. Remove from pan and keep warm. Stir flour into pan and cook for 3 minutes, add stock, wine, thyme and tomato paste, stirring until thickened. Add kidneys and onions, season to taste and heat through. Sprinkle with chopped parsley and serve over noodles.

Sliced mushrooms may be cooked with the kidneys if liked. The same recipe can be followed using liver instead of kidney. Serves 4.

CALVES' LIVER IN CREAM SAUCE
(KALBSLEBER)

If you should be in Rapperswil on a Tuesday you will
enjoy a speciality for that day of the week, calves' liver
in cream sauce, which I have never been able to get
there on any other day. This is because the butchers kill
on Monday, and local housewives almost queue-up for
liver next day. This is a dish worth queueing for.

1 lb fresh calves' liver
¼ cup flour
salt and pepper
½ teaspoon paprika

1 tablespoon chopped chives
   or parsley
2 tablespoons butter or fat
¼ cup dry white wine
½ cup cream

Pour hot water over liver and leave for 5 minutes, then
drain. Remove tubes and outer skin from liver and cut
into narrow slices. Combine flour, salt, pepper and
paprika in a paper bag and toss liver strips in flour until
well coated. Melt fat in pan and brown liver quickly
over fairly good heat, turning to brown both sides.
Lift from pan and keep hot. Pour wine into pan,
scraping the crust remaining in pan and blend well.
Remove from heat and add cream slowly, mix well and
heat, but do not allow to boil. Season if necessary, add
chives or parsley, then add liver. Re-heat if necessary
and serve with buttered noodles or spaetzli (page 155).

GRILLED CALVES' LIVER
(ZÜRCHER LEBERSPIESSLI)

When in Zürich every traveller interested in food should dine at one of the old Guild Houses facing the river. A number of these, with their fine panelling and decorations, and the shields of the various Guilds embossed on the windows, have been converted into restaurants, where good cooking and particularly good Swiss specialities are served.

This is a typical Zürich dish you will enjoy at the Guild Houses.

2 *lbs liver*
20 *sage leaves*
   (*or powdered sage*)
pepper

4–5 *rashers bacon*
2 *oz butter or margarine*
3 *tablespoons meat stock*

Remove skin and tubes from liver, and cover with water to stand for 5 minutes. Drain well and cut in thin slices, then into 1½-inch strips. Sprinkle each strip with pepper and place ½ sage leaf on each strip, or sprinkle lightly with dried sage. Cut bacon into strips the same size as liver and roll each piece of liver in a strip of bacon. Thread on skewers, placing 5 or 6 pieces on each skewer.

Melt butter in frying pan without browning. Arrange filled skewers in pan and cover, cooking over medium heat for about 10 to 12 minutes, turning once. Pour hot stock over liver and cook for another 2 or 3 minutes, then serve on heated dish.

Rösti (page 43) should be served with this dish.

BAKED LIVER AND ONIONS
(GEBACKENE LEBER MIT ZWIEBELN)

6 *slices calves' liver*   1 *bay leaf*
2 *large onions*   1 *teaspoon chopped fresh*
2 *oz butter*   *thyme*
½ *cup dry red wine*   *flour*
1 *tablespoon chopped parsley*   *salt and pepper*

Cut onions into ½-inch slices and separate the rings.
Place in ovenproof casserole with 1 oz butter, wine,
parsley, bay leaf, thyme, salt and pepper and ½ cup
water. Cover and bake in moderate oven (350 deg F or
No 5) for 30 minutes. Coat liver with flour, place on
top of onion slices and dot with remaining butter.
Cover and bake for 30 minutes, basting two or three
times with sauce in casserole. Remove cover and continue baking for another 10 minutes.
This is good served with spaetzli (page 155).

HUNTSMAN'S PIE

This is one way of using up any left-over meat to make
a tasty meal. The use of onions and apples with meat is
quite usual in many parts of Switzerland.

1 *lb cooked meat*   ½ *pint stock*
2 *lb cooked potatoes*   4 *oz breadcrumbs*
2 *onions*   2 *oz butter*
2 *large cooking apples*   *salt, pepper and nutmeg*

Mince or finely chop the meat, dice the potatoes, slice
onions very thin, and peel and slice the apples.

Put alternate layers of potatoes, meat, onion and apple in a deep casserole, beginning and ending with a layer of potatoes. Season with salt, pepper and nutmeg, taking into account that the stock is probably seasoned. Pour the stock over the layers, then sprinkle top with breadcrumbs and dot with small pieces of butter. Bake in a moderate oven (350 deg F or No 5) for 1 hour.

CHICKEN WITH CHEESE SAUCE
(HUHN MIT KÄSESAUCE)

1 *chicken approx 2–2½ lbs*	½ *pint milk*
8 *oz rice*	¼ *pint cream*
2 *oz butter*	*salt and pepper*
1 *oz cornflour*	6 *triangles Gruyère cheese*
chopped parsley	1 *small tin asparagus*

Boil chicken in the usual way, strain off stock and cut chicken into pieces. Cook rice in the boiling chicken stock, adding more water if necessary. Heat the milk and when boiling stir in cornflour blended with a little milk, stirring until smooth and thickened. Add butter, chopped cheese, salt and pepper to taste, and stir for 5 minutes over low heat until cheese has melted. Remove from stove and stir in cream and asparagus cut in pieces (keeping back 6 whole stalks for garnishing). Arrange rice round edge of a warmed serving plate, place chicken pieces in the middle and cover with cheese sauce. Garnish with asparagus pieces and chopped parsley. To serve 4–5.

DEVILLED CHICKEN
(POLLO 'AL DIAVOLO')

A tasty dish in the Ticino style.

2 lb chicken

butter and oil

2–3 oz chopped bacon

few leaves rosemary and sage

salt and pepper

1 tablespoon vinegar

Cut chicken in halves through the breastbone and flatten each piece well. Cook bacon in a mixture of butter and oil in a flameproof casserole for a few minutes then add herbs and place chicken pieces breast downwards on herbs and bacon. Season well. Cover with lid slightly smaller than casserole and place weight on top to keep chicken flattened. Cook fairly quickly for 5 minutes. Now turn chicken halves in casserole, cover and cook gently until tender. Remove from casserole to heated platter, add vinegar to juices in pan, cook quickly for 2 minutes then strain over chicken and serve at once.

CHICKEN SALAD WITH LEMON
(HÜHNERSALAT MIT ZITRONE)

8–10 oz cold, cooked chicken

1 lemon, sliced

1 dessertspoon lemon juice

2 tablespoons olive oil

3 teaspoons vinegar

1 bay leaf

2 tomatoes, sliced

1 lettuce

1 hard-boiled egg

salt and pepper

mayonnaise

Cut chicken into slices and place in earthenware dish. Cover with lemon slices. Make a marinade with olive oil, lemon juice, vinegar, bay leaf, salt and pepper and pour over chicken. Leave for 2 hours, turning once in the marinade. When ready to serve, drain chicken pieces. Put a layer of lettuce leaves in a shallow salad bowl, a layer of tomato slices then half the chicken pieces. Repeat these layers, finishing with chicken pieces. Garnish with alternate slices of egg and lemon (from the marinade), and serve mayonnaise separately.

An alternative recipe for this dish, which I enjoyed in St Gall, is to use cooked duck instead of chicken, and substitute orange slices and orange juice for lemon in the above recipe. A longer time in the marinade doesn't do it any harm, either. Serve in a dish lined with lettuce leaves, and garnish with alternate slices of tomato and orange.

RISOTTO WITH CHICKEN LIVERS
(RISOTTO AU FOIE DE VOLAILLE)

1 *onion, chopped*	2 *rashers bacon*
5 *oz butter*	1 *small carrot, sliced*
8 *oz rice*	1 *small onion, sliced*
salt and pepper	$\frac{3}{4}$ *oz flour*
1$\frac{1}{2}$ *pints chicken stock*	$\frac{3}{4}$ *pint stock (extra)*
2 *tablespoons dry white wine*	*juice of a lemon*
$\frac{1}{2}$ *lb chicken livers*	

If it is necessary to wash the rice, drain it well and spread out on a large platter to dry, turning with a fork at intervals. Sauté the chopped onion in 2 oz butter in a thick pan until transparent. Add the rice and keep turning with a fork for about 2 minutes. Add the chicken stock (make it with bouillon cubes if necessary) and season to taste. Simmer over low heat for 20 minutes, turning occasionally with a fork, until stock has been absorbed.

While rice is cooking prepare the sauce by melting
1 oz butter in a frying pan and frying the chopped
bacon, carrot and onion until lightly browned. Stir in
the flour and cook over low heat until lightly browned.
Stir in the extra stock and sherry and simmer very
gently until wanted.

Cover chicken livers with cold water and leave for
5 minutes, then drain well and cut in pieces. In a small
pan melt 2 oz butter and fry chicken livers for few
minutes. Season to taste and cook for another 2–3
minutes. Remove from pan and keep hot. Add lemon
juice to the pan and stir round, then strain in the sauce
and add chicken livers, re-heating without boiling.
Arrange rice in a ring on a heated platter and serve
chicken livers in the rice ring. Garnish with parsley and
lemon slices.

ROAST GOOSE WITH PRUNES

This is a dish for a festive occasion, as served in the
German part of Switzerland.

8–10 *lb goose*	*salt and pepper to taste*
2 *cooking apples*	1 *tablespoon butter*
1 *large orange*	1 *cup boiling water*
18 *prunes, soaked until tender*	¾ *cup dry white wine*
2 *leaves of sage*	

Clean bird, wash well inside and out, and dry well.
Sprinkle inside with salt and pepper. Peel, core and
chop apples; slice orange without peeling; remove
stones from 6 prunes, chop and mix with other fruit.
Use this mixture to stuff bird, adding sage leaves. Close
vent and neck opening and tie wings and legs firmly to
body.

Melt butter in baking tin, place goose on one side on a rack in dish and roast 1 hour in a hot oven (425 deg F or No 8–9) until well browned, then turn on other side to roast for another hour, reducing heat to moderate (375 deg F or No 6). The bird should be basted frequently with the water and wine mixed with the butter in tin.

When bird is tender, remove from baking tin and keep hot. Make gravy with juices in the tin, serve goose garnished with remainder of prunes.

The fruit from inside the goose should not be served, as it is only used to add flavour to the bird.

MARINATED PIGEONS
(PICCIONI ALLA MARINARA)

This is a recipe from the Ticino district, and when pigeons are not available, small chickens can be used.

2 *pigeons or small chickens*   2 *beaten eggs*
1 *cup olive oil*   *browned breadcrumbs*
1 *tablespoon lemon juice*   *sprigs of parsley*
salt and pepper   *butter*
  dry white wine

Cut birds in halves through breastbone and flatten each half well. Arrange in a single layer in an earthenware dish. Mix oil, lemon juice, salt, pepper and parsley and pour over birds. Turn after one hour and leave for another hour. When ready to cook, drain birds, dip into beaten egg, then into breadcrumbs, coating well. Heat butter in baking dish and brown birds well, then place in moderate oven and bake for about 30 minutes, basting with marinade at intervals. When birds are cooked, remove to heated serving dish, add a little white wine to juices in pan and boil up quickly, then pour over birds. To serve 4.

PIGEONS LOCARNO
(PICCIONI 'ALLA LOCARNO')

It is only a steamer trip over the blue waters of Lake Maggiore from Switzerland to Italy, so it is natural that Italian style cooking should be popular with local people and tourists alike. This is a good example of the tasty dishes you can enjoy in this part of the country, and which can be made in your own kitchen. If pigeons are not available, try young chicken breasts.

4 young pigeons	fresh sage leaves
¼ lb lean smoked ham, sliced	stale bread cut 1-inch thick
¼ lb small button mushrooms	olive oil
garlic	melted butter
salt and pepper	4 metal skewers

With a sharp knife, carefully remove the pigeon breasts, cut each into four pieces and season with salt and pepper. Cut ham into 1-inch squares. Rub the bread over with a cut clove of garlic and cut into 1-inch cubes. Thread ingredients on to skewers, alternating a bread cube, slice of ham, sage leaf, pigeon and mushroom, until skewers are full. Soak in olive oil for 5 minutes, turning to cover all sides with the oil, then drain and place on a rack in baking tin in a very hot oven (425 deg F or No 8) and cook until browned and cooked through, basting occasionally with melted butter, and turning once or twice.

Serve on a bed of cooked rice, accompanied by a green salad. For 6.

BRAISED PARTRIDGES
(PERDRIX BRAISÉE)

During the season, wild fowl figures prominently in many menus in Switzerland, and this dish of partridges is a good choice.

2 *plump partridges*	1 *pint clear stock*
2 *large carrots*	*(bouillon cubes may be used)*
1 *turnip*	*salt and pepper to taste*
2 *onions*	*bouquet garni*
1 *rasher of bacon*	*¼ lb small mushrooms*
2 *oz butter*	*chopped parsley*
	flour

Clean and dress the partridges. Dice the vegetables and bacon. Brown the partridges in the butter, turning to brown on all sides, then remove from pan. Fry the vegetables and bacon in same pan, adding a little more butter if necessary, until golden brown. Place vegetables in greased casserole, add bouquet garni and place birds on bed of vegetables. Season to taste and pour stock round. Cover and cook in moderate oven (350 deg F or No 5) for about 30 minutes. The birds should not be overcooked. Remove from casserole and keep hot. Cook mushrooms in a little butter for 5 or 6 minutes and keep hot. Strain liquor from casserole and thicken with a little flour, cooking until smooth and thickened stirring all the time, then cook for 5 minutes. Pour gravy round the birds and garnish with mushrooms sprinkled with chopped parsley.

VENISON WITH CHESTNUTS

During the hunting season menus in both private houses and hotels feature excellent game dishes. Pride of place is given to venison, both roebuck and stag, and to chamois which only has a short season during the autumn. The following venison dish from the Canton of the Grisons is delicious and could be made by any housewife, but the famous saddle of venison *à la mode des Grisons* is more of a luxury and a dish to be ordered from a restaurant during the season.

1½ *lb venison*
1 *cup red wine*
1 *large onion, chopped*
1 *bay leaf*
½ *cinnamon stick*
3 *tablespoons butter*

¼ *teaspoon dried marjoram or thyme*
1 *tomato, peeled and chopped*
12 *chestnuts, peeled (see page 121)*
1 *cup beef stock*
salt and black pepper
flour

The day before it is to be cooked put venison in a bowl with onion, bay leaf, cinnamon and wine. Cover and leave in cool place for at least 12 hours, turning occasionally. When ready to cook, strain off marinade into a saucepan and boil until slightly reduced. Cut venison into cubes and cook in butter with the onion until lightly browned. Add salt and pepper, marjoram, tomato, marinade, stock and chestnuts. Cover and simmer for 40 minutes or until meat is tender. If necessary thicken gravy with a little flour blended with water, stirring until required consistency.

Serve with spaetzli (page 155). To serve 4.

VENISON GOULASH
(WILDGULASCH)

In autumn when venison is in season, this is another way of cooking it.

1½ to 2 *lb venison*
4 *oz streaky belly-pork*
4 *tomatoes, peeled*
3 or 4 *juniper berries*
1 *bay leaf*
1 *tablespoon flour*
1½ *pints mixed beef stock and water*

3 *onions, sliced*
salt and pepper
1 *cup small fried mushrooms* OR
1 *small tin champignons*
½ *cup red wine*

Cut venison in serving pieces. Cube the pork and put into a hot pan to start fat to melt. Add a little extra pork fat if necessary. Brown venison in fat, turning to brown on all sides, then add onions and brown lightly. Add tomatoes, berries, bay leaf, stock and water and season to taste. Cover and simmer until meat is tender. Blend flour with wine and stir into mixture, then add mushrooms and stir until slightly thickened. Cook for a few minutes.

Serve with buttered noodles and mixed pickles, or with rice.

HARE À LA GRISONS

The wide range of game animals and birds available in the mountainous country of the Grisons adds variety to menus over the winter months, and hare is a popular dish. Like most game dishes it is first marinaded for at least 12 hours before cooking. Only the legs and saddle of the hare are used for this.

required amount of hare
strips of bacon
½ pint white wine
½ cup wine vinegar
1 large onion, sliced
olive oil
salt and whole peppercorns

mixed herbs such as thyme,
*   tarragon and rosemary*
1 bay leaf, crumbled
1 tablespoon French mustard
1 tablespoon tomato paste
flour
fresh or sour cream
1 tablespoon chopped parsley

Wipe and trim the hare meat, carefully cutting away the small tail bone at the base of the back legs, and removing the small end bones of the legs if possible. Lard the pieces with thin strips of bacon and place in an earthenware dish. Make the marinade with wine, vinegar, herbs, bay leaf, chopped onion and peppercorns and pour over the meat. Stand in a cool place for 12 hours, turning the meat several times. When ready to cook, drain the meat well, and strain the marinade. Heat some oil in a fairly large saucepan and brown the meat on all sides. Mix mustard and tomato paste with half the marinade liquor and add, season to taste and cook gently for about 1 hour, or until meat is tender. When cooked, remove meat to a heated dish and keep hot. Blend flour with a little of the marinade and stir into the gravy in pan and boil for a few minutes. Remove from heat and stir in cream. Serve over hare.

CARROT AND ALMOND PIE
(AARGAUER KUCHEN)

5 *eggs, separated*
8 *oz castor sugar*
juice and grated rind ½ lemon
8 *oz peeled and crushed almonds*
8 *oz raw carrots, grated*

1 *teaspoon cinnamon*
¼ *teaspoon grated nutmeg*
1½ *oz flour*
1 *tablespoon kirsch or rum*

Beat egg yolks with 6 oz sugar and grated lemon rind. Add almonds, carrots and lemon juice, then the flour and kirsch, blending well. Beat egg whites until stiff and fold into carrot mixture, mixing well. Turn into a well buttered pie dish and bake in a moderate oven (350 deg F or No 5) for about 1 hour, or until firm and set. Dust top with remainder of sugar, and serve either hot or cold.

SUGAR TART
(ZUCKERWÄHE)

short pastry
4 *eggs*
2 *oz melted butter*

½ *cup castor sugar*
½ *teaspoon cinnamon*
1 *oz butter (extra)*

Line a sandwich tin with pastry. Beat eggs with 1 tablespoon sugar and pour into pastry case. Pour melted butter over the eggs and bake in a moderate oven until pastry is golden and custard set. Blend extra butter with remaining sugar and cinnamon and sprinkle over the top of the filling, then return to oven just until topping has melted a little.

STUFFED APPLES

This recipe comes from the high Alpine valleys where beachnuts and walnuts are grown in profusion. It makes a pleasant change from the usual baked apples.

6 *large cooking apples*　　1 *egg white*
½ *cup finely chopped nuts*　2 *tablespoons butter or*
½ *cup sugar*　　　　　　　　*margarine*

Wash and core apples. Mix nuts, sugar and egg white together, blending well. Fill apple centres with this mixture, and stand them in an ovenproof dish. Melt butter and pour round the apples. Bake in a fairly hot oven (375 deg F or No 6) basting occasionally while they are baking. Be careful the apples do not split, and if cooking too much on top, cover with a piece of foil or buttered paper.

Serve with cream or custard.

APPLE CAKE

Pumpernickel bread is used for this recipe, but if unobtainable, a dark malt bread could be used. The bread should be several days old.

10–12 *slices pumpernickel bread* 4 *oz melted butter*
2–3 *lb tart cooking apples*   *whipped cream*
4–6 *oz brown sugar*

Cut off the crusts and crumble the bread roughly. Peel and slice the apples. Butter an ovenproof dish and put in a layer of crumbled bread sprinkled with sugar. Pour melted butter over this layer, then arrange a layer of sliced apples sprinkled with sugar. Repeat these layers until all ingredients are used up, finishing with a layer of apples and sugar. Bake in a moderate oven (350 deg F or No 5) for about 45 minutes, or until apples are cooked through. Serve hot, covered with a layer of whipped cream.

APPLE TART
(APFELWÄHE)

rich short pastry   1 *teaspoon flour*
2 *lb tart cooking apples* 5 *oz sugar*
2 *eggs*   *pinch cinnamon*
¼ *pint top milk or cream*

Peel and core apples and cut into eighths. Sprinkle with 2 oz sugar and leave for a few minutes. Roll out pastry and line a 10-inch pie plate, finishing the edge with a double roll and crimp with a fork and thumb. Arrange apple slices evenly on the pastry, overlapping in circles. Bake in a hot oven (425 deg F or No 8) for 20 minutes.

Make a custard with the beaten eggs, cream or milk, flour, sugar and cinnamon and gently pour over the apples. Lower oven temperature to moderate and continue baking pie until custard is set when tested with a knife. Be careful not to let the custard boil or it will curdle.

LATTICE APPLE TART

short pastry   1 tablespoon lemon juice
4 medium cooking apples   ½ oz butter
2 tablespoons honey   egg for glazing

Roll out pastry and line a 9-inch pie plate. Flute the edges. Peel, core and slice the apples and put into saucepan with lemon juice and butter. Cover and simmer until tender. Beat well with a wooden spoon, then add honey which has been melted over hot water. Cool slightly, then pour into pastry-lined plate. Roll out pastry trimmings and cut into strips, placing four each way over the filling to form a lattice, securing to sides of tart. Brush edges and lattice over with a little egg to glaze. Bake in a moderately hot oven (375 deg F or No 6) for 25–30 minutes.

APPLE AND RICE MERINGUE
(POMMES AU RIZ)

4 oz rice   pinch salt
1 pint milk   2–3 drops vanilla essence
8 oz sugar   1 egg yolk
1 pint water   2 egg whites
2 lb medium cooking apples   apricot conserve

Wash the rice well and cook in a double saucepan with the milk until tender and milk is absorbed. Add 3 oz sugar and cool. Make a syrup with water and 4 oz sugar and bring to boil. Peel and core 4 evenly-sized apples and cook in the syrup until just soft, but be careful not to overcook or they will break. Lift out with a slotted spoon and leave to cool. Peel and slice remainder of apples and cook in same syrup until reduced to a pulp. Beat until smooth, then add vanilla and cooked rice. When cool add the slightly beaten egg yolk and pour mixture into a large ovenproof dish.

Carefully place the four cooked apples in the rice, leaving about 1-inch of the apple above the top of the rice. Fill centres of apples with apricot (or strawberry) conserve. Beat egg whites with pinch salt and remainder of sugar until stiff and pile roughly on tops of apples, bringing meringue down the apples to top of rice to seal them. Put into a fairly hot oven just long enough to set the meringue and tint a pale golden.

APPLE FRITTERS

Fritters of all kinds are very popular in Switzerland, and other fruits can be fried and cooked in the same way. Make a batter as given on page 83, adding a little sugar.

Peel, core and slice the apples, or cut into cubes if preferred. Put into a shallow dish and just cover with sweet white wine, leaving for some hours until ready to cook. Drain well, coat with batter and drop by spoonfuls into hot oil or butter, frying until crisp and golden brown. Drain on absorbent paper and sprinkle with a mixture of castor sugar and cinnamon. Serve at once, garnished with lemon quarters.

CHERRY BUNCHES

Swiss cherries are delicious eaten cooked or raw, and they are especially good prepared like this.

Tie 5 or 6 cherries together in bunches by their stalks. Dip into sweet batter (page 83) and fry in deep hot oil or butter until crisp and golden. Drain and serve at once, sprinkled with castor sugar, allowing 2 or 3 bunches for each serve.

RICE FRITTERS

3 oz rice
1 pint milk
2 oz butter
1 tablespoon raisins or
    sultanas
pinch salt

1 dessertspoon sugar
little grated lemon rind
1 tablespoon brandy or rum
3 eggs, separated
2 oz flour
oil or fat for frying

Pour boiling water over raisins or sultanas and stand for 5 minutes, then drain and spread out on paper to dry. Cook well-washed rice in milk for 20 minutes, stirring with a fork occasionally. Add butter, raisins, salt, sugar and lemon rind, mix well, then cool. Add rum or brandy, beaten egg yolks, flour, and mix well, then allow to stand for several hours. Just before frying, beat egg whites until stiff and fold into rice mixture. Heat oil or fat and drop spoonfuls of the mixture into the hot pan, frying until crisp and golden brown. Drain on absorbent paper and serve at once.

Sprinkle with a little castor sugar and serve with lemon quarters

CHEESECAKE
(KÄSEKUCHEN)

There are a number of different kinds of cheesecakes
served in various parts of Switzerland. This one comes
from the Lucerne district.

FOR THE PASTRY:

6 *oz flour*
pinch salt
3 *oz butter*

1 *teaspoon castor sugar*
1 *egg yolk*

FOR THE FILLING:

2 *oz butter*
3 *oz castor sugar*
2 *eggs, separated*
1½ *oz ground almonds*

8 *oz cottage cheese*
1 *oz semolina*
2 *oz seeded raisins*
1 *lemon*

Sift flour and salt into basin and rub in butter until
mixture resembles fine breadcrumbs. Add sugar and
mix to a firm paste with beaten egg yolk, adding a little
water if necessary. Roll out on lightly floured board and
line a sandwich tin, one with a removable base if you
have one. Press down well to remove any air bubbles
and trim edges neatly.

Make the filling by creaming butter and sugar together until light and fluffy. Grate rind of lemon and
squeeze out juice. Mix lightly beaten egg yolks with
ground almonds, cottage cheese, semolina, chopped
raisins, grated rind and juice of lemon. Fold into
creamed butter and sugar, then fold in stiffly beaten
egg whites. Turn filling into pastry-lined tin and bake
in moderately slow oven (325 deg F or No 4) for 50 to
60 minutes, or until pastry is pale golden and filling is
set. Remove from tin and serve cold.

CHESTNUT CAKES

There are many chestnut trees in various parts of the country, and the local housewives use them in many ways. These 'cakes' can be served as a vegetable, or sugar can be added and they are then served as a sweet. Either way they are very acceptable.

1 *lb chestnuts*	4 *oz flour*
2 *eggs*	*browned breadcrumbs*
salt and pepper or sugar and nutmeg	2 *oz butter or margarine*

Split each chestnut shell with a sharp knife, cover with water and boil until they are soft, then remove shells and brown skin. Put through a food mill or fairly coarse sieve. Mix with 1 beaten egg, salt and pepper (or sugar and nutmeg), and form into flat cakes. Coat with flour, lightly beaten egg, and then in breadcrumbs and fry in the hot butter or margarine, turning to brown on both sides.

As a supper dish they are good served with a well flavoured cheese sauce, or as a sweet serve with jam thinned with a little fruit juice or red wine.

GATEAU D'OEUFS A LA NEIGE

Geneva is a very cosmopolitan city, where many countries have inspired the cuisine, but French cooking is generally served in the homes. It is a gracious city, set on the shores of Lac Léman, and from there to Montreux villages and towns are strung like beads on a thread bordering the lake, each one of which is worth a visit. France is visible on the other side of the lake, and steamers scurry backwards and forwards over the blue waters, calling at many of the most charming and populous centres.

I have had many excellent meals in Geneva, and one of the recipes I collected there was this unusual and delicious dessert.

4 *eggs, separated*   6 *oz granulated sugar*
½ *pint milk*   *pinch salt*
8 *oz castor sugar*   3 *tablespoons water*
½ *teaspoon vanilla essence*

Beat egg yolks slightly in the top of a double saucepan, then add milk and 2 oz castor sugar. Cook over hot water until custard is thick enough to coat the back of a spoon, stirring all the time. Add vanilla and keep custard hot without allowing the water underneath to boil.

Heat a spotlessly clean 7-inch cake tin in the oven. Heat the granulated sugar and water together in a small, thick saucepan over moderate heat, stirring until sugar is completely dissolved, then bring to the boil and allow to cook gently, without stirring, until a deep golden colour. Pour this caramel into the hot cake tin, running it quickly over the bottom and sides of the tin, coating it well. Put aside for a few minutes to set. Beat egg whites until stiff, beat in salt and 1 tablespoon of remaining castor sugar, then gently fold in remainder of sugar, blending in evenly. Spoon this meringue into the caramel-lined tin, and place in a fairly hot oven (375 deg F or No 6) for 25 to 30 minutes, until it is risen and pale golden, and fairly firm. Remove from oven and immediately turn out on a serving dish, caramel side upwards. Pour custard sauce round (not over) the meringue and serve either hot or cold.

ICE CREAM
WITH CHERRY SAUCE

Half-way between Zürich and Lucerne is the town of
Zug, on the lake of the same name, home of the famous
and delicious kirschtorte, a cake flavoured with kirsch
which is rather too complicated to give you here. But I
will always remember Zug for a dish of ice cream with a
wonderful cherry sauce – also flavoured with kirsch –
which you could make at home.

3 oz sugar	4 teaspoons redcurrant jelly
¼ pint water	1 tablespoon kirsch
1 lb stoned red cherries	ice cream

Heat sugar and water together until sugar is dissolved.
Add cherries and simmer until tender, then drain off
the juice. Add jelly to cherry juice and cook until thick.
Pour kirsch over cherries and leave while sauce is cool-
ing. Put portions of ice cream into 6 small individual
dishes, arrange cherries round and pour sauce over the
top.

CHOCOLATE-ALMOND CREME

4 oz dark chocolate	4 oz ground almonds
1 tablespoon top milk	2 oz castor sugar
4 oz softened butter	¼ pint whipping cream

Grate chocolate and melt over hot water in the top
milk. Beat in the ground almonds, butter and sugar.
Whip cream and fold chocolate mixture into it until
smooth. Pour into serving bowl, or individual dishes and
leave in cool place until set. Serve with fresh sponge
fingers.

BROKEN BATTER PUDDING
(KOHLERMUS)

4 *eggs, separated*
2 *oz castor sugar*
about 1 *pint milk*
8 *oz flour*

3 *oz lard or butter*
pinch salt
extra sugar

Beat egg yolks and castor sugar together, then add milk, flour and salt, and beat well to get a smooth batter. Beat egg whites until stiff and fold into batter. Heat lard in a baking tin until really hot, then quickly pour in batter. Bake in a moderately hot oven for 20 minutes. Very carefully, with a wide spatula or egg lift, turn the pudding over in the tin, and bake for another 15 minutes or until well browned on both sides. Turn out of tin and break into small, irregular pieces. Sprinkle with sugar, or serve with a sauce made with crushed berries or sieved fruit.

Another version of this pudding is fried instead of baked. The butter is heated in a thick pan and the batter poured in. As the batter fries it is cut into pieces and turned until golden brown all over.

RASPBERRY VACHERIN

Neuchâtel is not only the watchmaking centre of Switzerland, it is also the centre of a good wine-making district (*see* page 11) and the shores of Lake Neuchâtel are terraced with vineyards.

Every year at vintage time (usually late September or early October) the townspeople celebrate the grape harvest with a colourful and gay wine festival, with wonderful floats in procession, a confetti battle, and dancing in the streets, with everybody from town councillors to street sweepers enjoying the fun (even though the street sweepers have a terrific job next day clearing up the mess left after the celebrations).

Part of the festival are several official dinners, and when I visited Neuchâtel for the vintage, I had ample opportunity to sample both the excellent food and the wines of the district. This delicious dessert was served at one dinner, and I obtained the recipe – after much persuasion. If you have a deep freeze you can make the vacherin up with any fruits in season, then freeze to serve at any time of the year.

4 egg whites
7 oz castor sugar
3 oz plain flour
2 oz butter, melted

1 lb raspberries
3 oz ground hazelnuts
    (other nuts may be used)
double cream or ice cream

Whip egg whites until stiff, fold in sugar, flour, ground nuts, and cooled melted butter. Grease and flour three shallow sandwich tins (with removable bases if possible) and spread the mixture thinly in the prepared tins. Bake in moderate oven until pale golden and firm. Remove from tins immediately and when cool sandwich together with fruit mixed with cream or ice cream.

BRANDIED CHERRIES
WITH CREAMED CHEESE

Rich creamy desserts are first favourites with Swiss housewives who are accustomed to using the best quality dairy products. This delicious combination of cherries, cream, cheese and brandy comes from Lucerne, where I first tasted it one night for dinner in a garden overlooking the lake. It is a sweet for a special occasion, and is so rich that only a small portion should be served, the amounts given here serving 8 people.

1 lb cottage cheese

2½ cups canned or stewed cherries

1 cup whipping cream

½ cup brandy

Press cottage cheese through a coarse sieve to break up curds. Line a strainer with cheesecloth or fine muslin, put cheese in strainer, set over bowl and refrigerate overnight to drain off whey. Combine cherries (dark ones are best) and juice with brandy in a saucepan and cook quickly until boiling. Remove from heat, cover and leave until cold. Chill until ready to serve. Whip cream until stiff. Break up drained cottage cheese with a fork and add to cream, stirring lightly with fork until blended. Pile on a serving dish and arrange cherries around it, spooning a little of the juice over each serve.

This same cottage cheese and cream mixture can be served with strawberries which have been soaked overnight in brandy. Add a little sugar to taste.

WINE CUSTARD
(CRÊME CUITE AU VIN)

2 tablespoons white wine   ½ cup sugar
2 tablespoons water   1 teaspoon grated lemon rind
1½ tablespoons lemon juice   3 egg yolks

Place water, wine, lemon juice and sugar in small pan
and heat just long enough to dissolve sugar. Add lemon
rind and remove from heat. Beat egg yolks and add
2 tablespoons of wine mixture, stirring in gradually.
When blended stir into remainder of wine mixture in
saucepan and stir over very low heat until mixture
thickens and coats the spoon. Remove from heat and
stir until cooled. It will thicken as it cools. Serve well
chilled with strawberries or other fruit.

VANILLA CREAM SAUCE

This is one of the rich and creamy sauces which are
served with strawberries or other berry fruits in season,
and which are very popular with both tourists and local
people alike.

1 cup whipping cream   ⅔ cup castor sugar
3 egg yolks   ¾ teaspoon vanilla essence

Whip cream until stiff. Beat egg yolks while slowly
adding sugar and vanilla, beating until light and foamy.
Fold in the whipped cream and chill slightly before
serving with fruit.

MERINGUE TART

Either of the two preceding recipes can be used as filling for a meringue case made with the whites of three eggs and 6 oz castor sugar. Beat the egg whites until stiff, then slowly beat in half the sugar, then add remainder of sugar all at once and fold in. Pipe into an 8-inch round on oiled paper, hollowing out the middle, then bake in a very cool oven for about 1½ hours. Cool and fill as desired.

CHESTNUT PUDDING
(MONT BLANC)

Chestnuts grow well in many parts of Switzerland, and are used in a number of ways, but this classic pudding is a great favourite, just as it is in the neighbouring countries of France and Italy. Called after the famous mountain, the pudding must be made in the shape of a cone, and should be kept as light as possible in texture.

1 lb chestnuts	pinch salt
½ lb sugar	4 oz whipping cream
milk	marsala wine or brandy

With a pointed knife score the chestnuts across the rounded side, cover with water and boil for 10–15 minutes. Drain, cool until they can be handled (but while still hot), remove shell and inner skins. Put into a thick saucepan, cover with milk and cook slowly, covered, until chestnuts are tender, probably about 1 hour. Drain well and mash with sugar and salt. If you have a food mill use it for this, otherwise a coarse strainer will do. Holding the strainer over the serving dish, press the mashed chestnuts through to form a mound or cone on the dish. Whip the cream, adding a little marsala or brandy to flavour if desired, then lightly pour over the chestnut cone. The pudding will be lighter if the desired shape can be made without pressing it down or shaping it after sieving. Serve as soon as possible. For 4–6.

LEMON CHIFFON CREAM
(ZITRONENCRÈME)

4 eggs, separated   juice of 2 lemons
½ cup sugar   ½ cup dry white wine
grated rind 1 small lemon

Beat egg yolks and sugar together until light and fluffy. Add lemon rind and gradually stir in lemon juice and wine, blending well but lightly. Pour into top of double saucepan over hot but not boiling water, and stir until mixture thickens. Be very careful not to allow it to boil. Cool slightly.

Beat egg whites until stiff enough to hold peaks, then fold into lemon cream. Turn into serving dish and chill.

When available, strawberries may be used to garnish this dish, but it is quite delicious as it is.

STUFFED PEACHES
(PESCHE RIPIENE)

6 large, ripe peaches   2 tablespoons sugar
3 oz almond macaroons   1 oz butter
1 egg yolk   3 tablespoons marsala wine

Do not peel peaches but cut them in halves and remove the stones, also a little of the pulp to make a larger centre space. Crush the macaroons and mix with other ingredients, then stuff peaches with the mixture, smoothing over the top evenly. Place in a well buttered ovenproof dish and bake in a moderate oven for about 30 minutes, pouring the wine round the peaches but not over them, for the last 15 minutes.

KRUMMEL TORTE

During the winter, when fruits are unobtainable, Alpine housewives use fruits they have dried in the summer, combined with nuts which grow in the region. Many and varied are these cakes and tarts, and much appreciated by those with a sweet tooth. This is one which can be served as a dessert or a cake, as desired.

½ cup seeded raisins
1 cup pre-soaked dried apricots
½ cup chopped nuts
¾ cup sweet white wine
2 eggs

1 cup sugar
½ cup fine dry breadcrumbs
pinch salt
1½ teaspoons baking powder
whipped cream

Grease a 9-inch cake tin and line bottom with paper. Chop apricots and add with raisins and nuts to saucepan with wine. Simmer 10 minutes, stirring occasionally. Allow to cool. Beat eggs with sugar until light and creamy. Mix crumbs, salt and baking powder and stir into eggs, then stir in cooked fruit, blending all well together. Turn into prepared tin and bake in moderate oven (350 deg F or No 5) for about 40 minutes. Cool in tin and turn out on serving plate. Spread with a layer of sweetened whipped cream and garnish with coarsely chopped nuts or glacé cherries.

PRUNES IN RED WINE

1 lb dried prunes
½ pint red wine
2 oz castor sugar

½-inch vanilla bean
boiling water
cream cheese or yoghourt

Wash prunes well if necessary, then just cover with boiling water and stand for about 1 hour. Bring to boil in same water and cook for 20 minutes. Pour off half the liquid and put aside, then add vanilla bean, sugar and wine. Simmer very slowly for about 1 hour, or until prunes are quite tender, adding more liquid if necessary. When prunes are soft, pour off syrup, remove stones and press prunes through sieve or food mill. Add enough syrup to bring mixture to consistency of thick custard. Chill for several hours. Serve topped with yoghourt or cream cheese softened with a little of the prune syrup.

FRUIT CASSEROLE

¼ lb dried prunes
¼ lb dried apricots
4 oz sugar

2 good-sized cooking apples
1 teaspoon grated lemon rind
juice 1 lemon

Wash dried fruits and soak overnight in just enough water to cover. Place in ovenproof casserole with sugar and lemon juice, cover and cook in moderate oven until tender. Add peeled and sliced apples and lemon rind and cook for another 20–25 minutes until apples are tender. Serve hot with custard or cream.

FRUIT COMPÔTE

There is a plentitude of fruit growing in the valleys of the Valais Canton in the summer, and the housewives of the district make wonderful combinations of the various kinds of fruits as they are in season. This fruit salad was one of the best I have ever tasted, yet it was so simple anybody could make it, using whatever fresh fruits are available at the time.

2 tablespoons castor sugar	1 cup raspberries
1 cup water	1 cup strawberries
1 dessertspoon lemon juice	2 tablespoons kirsch or
1 cup stoned cherries	curaçao

Make a syrup of sugar, water and lemon juice and boil 5 minutes. Chill well. Prepare the fruit and place in serving bowl. When syrup is chilled, add liqueur and pour over fruit. Cover and chill for 1 to 2 hours. Serve with cream or yoghurt.

FRUIT SALAD
(MACEDOINE DE FRUITS)

1 small pineapple	1 lb strawberries
1 large orange	2 large, fresh peaches
1 lb raspberries	2 oz kirsch or muscatel

Mash the raspberries with the kirsch or wine and set aside. Peel, core and chop pineapple (if fresh pineapple is not available a small can of pineapple, well drained of syrup, may be used) ; peel and slice orange, peel and slice peaches, hull strawberries but leave whole. Place in a bowl and leave in a warm place for 1 hour. Pour off accumulated fruit juice (use next day for sauce or jelly), and cover fruit with prepared raspberries. Chill for several hours. If necessary, a little castor sugar may be added. Serve plain or with cream or ice cream.

RED PUDDING
(ROTE GRUTZE)

8 *oz raspberries*   4 *oz water*
8 *oz red currants*   6 *oz castor sugar*
8 *oz dark red cherries*   2 *oz cornflour*

Wash fruit well and stone cherries. Cook with water and sugar for 5 or 6 minutes until tender. Blend cornflour with a little water and stir into fruit mixture, stirring until smooth and thickened. Turn out into serving dish and chill until ready to serve. Cream or custard may be served with this.

Another version of this pudding directs for the stewed fruit to be pressed through a sieve before thickening. The amount of water required depends on juiciness of fruit and should be regulated to give a thick but not too stiff mixture.

FRUIT SOUP
(FRUCHTSUPPE)

Sweet soups are an unusual speciality of the Basle region. They are made with wine, with grape juice, cherries, mixed fruits and even with chocolate. This is a typical example.

1 *lb mixed fruit in season*	*sugar to taste*
1½ *pints water, or half water*	*butter*
and half wine	*1-inch cubes of day-old*
1 *rounded teaspoon cornflour*	*bread*

Prepare a mixture of ripe fruits such as peaches, apricots, cherries and pears, or whatever is available. Leave cherries whole if used, and peel and dice other fruits about the same size.

Cook fruit in water or wine mixture until tender, then sweeten to taste. Blend cornflour with a little water and stir into fruit, cooking for a few minutes and stirring all the time until slightly thickened. Fry the bread cubes in butter until crisp and golden, drain on absorbent paper and sprinkle with castor sugar. Serve fruit soup hot, garnished with bread croûtons.

This is usually served as a first course for dinner, but it can also be served as a pudding – personally, I prefer it as a pudding.

CHERRY CLAFOUTIS

Cherries are the traditional fruit to use for this pudding, but the same directions can be followed using other soft fruit such as apricots or berries.

1 *lb cherries*	2 *oz castor sugar*
3 *oz flour*	3 *eggs*
1 *pint milk*	

Wash cherries and remove stalks, dry them as much as possible, and put into a greased ovenproof dish. Blend milk into the flour, stirring until quite smooth. Add sugar and lightly beaten eggs and mix lightly but thoroughly. Pour this batter over the fruit. If cherries are rather sour, extra sugar may be needed.

Bake in a moderate oven (350 deg F or No 5) for 35–40 minutes, or until topping is set and golden brown on top. Serve hot or cold in the dish in which it is cooked, or leave to get cold and turn out with the cherries on top. Cream may be served with the pudding.

STOLLEN

This is a delicious cake-bread from Schaffhausen, and I ate far too many slices of it after visiting the spectacular Rhine falls. The sight of the thundering, tumbling waters must have given me an appetite, for I enjoyed my stollen and cups of creamy coffee very much.

4 tablespoons luke-warm milk	2 oz chopped almonds
2 oz sugar	3 oz candied peel, chopped
½ teaspoon salt	1 oz glacé cherries, sliced
½ oz fresh yeast	1 oz seedless raisins
2 oz melted butter	1 teaspoon grated lemon rind
½ lb plain flour	½ lb icing sugar
1 egg	1 teaspoon lemon juice

Using a large bowl mix milk, sugar and salt together, then crumble in the yeast, mixing well. Slowly blend in the flour, melted butter and beaten egg, then knead lightly but firmly to a smooth dough. Cover with a tea-towel and leave in a warm place to rise until doubled in bulk. Turn out on a lightly floured board and knead again, then pat dough into a circle. Mix cherries, nuts, raisins, candied peel and grated rind and sprinkle evenly over the dough. Knead the fruit into the dough, and turn into a well-greased 2-lb loaf tin. Bake in a moderate oven (350 deg F or No 5) for 35 minutes. Turn out of tin on to rack to cool. Mix sifted icing sugar until smooth with lemon juice and a little water and coat top of loaf with icing. Cut in slices to serve.

GATEAU AU VIN CUIT

This is a typical farmhouse recipe made for winter eating, either as a pudding or a cake. It needs long slow cooking, but it is worth the time it takes.

A mixture of peeled, sliced apples, pre-soaked prunes and seeded raisins is cooked in very little water until tender. Press the fruit through a sieve, add a little sweet red wine and simmer gently until very thick, stirring occasionally. The finished product should be almost like a paste. Sweeten to taste while still hot, then cool.

Line a 10-inch pie plate with short pastry and bake blind. Pour in the fruit mixture and serve at once if using as a pudding, or leave overnight to cool and dry out slightly if serving as a cake. It is delicious with cream, or with custard as a pudding.

There are several variations of this recipe, some districts using a mixture of dried apricots and prunes, others using apples and raisins only. I was first introduced to it in the hills above Montreux, on a cold rainy day while I waited for a train, and my hostess parcelled up a large slice of the gateau 'to keep out the cold'. I enjoyed it while watching the incredible twists and

turns taken by that little train over the mountains surrounding the lake, as we zig-zagged higher and higher,
and then ran down through the lovely Saanen Valley.
I always remember the gateau and the journey together
– so are memories made.

CHOCOLATE AND CREAM CAKE

Swiss chocolate is famous all over the world, deservedly
so as you will find after tasting some of the delicious
confections to be found in all parts of the country. As a
flavouring for cakes and desserts it is also popular, and
this example can be served as either a cake or a dessert,
as you please. It is best made overnight.

4 oz dark chocolate   1 egg yolk
½ pint milk   ½ pint whipping cream
3 oz butter   8 oz sponge fingers
4 oz castor sugar   nuts or grated chocolate

Grate or break chocolate into pieces and melt in half the
milk, blending until smooth and creamy, then stir in
remainder of milk. Cream butter and sugar thoroughly,
beat in egg yolk and lastly the chocolate milk mixture,
beating until smooth. Whip the cream until thick. Line
a square cake tin with greaseproof paper, pour in a
layer of the chocolate mixture, cover with sponge
fingers then with whipped cream. Repeat these layers,
finishing with layer of whipped cream. Chill overnight,
then turn out on serving plate.

The cake can be garnished with chopped nuts or
grated chocolate, or extra whipped cream can be piped
round the edge and sides if desired. Cut in small slices
to serve.

CHESTNUT CREAM CAKE

This is a rich cake which could also be served as a dessert. I first tasted this in Gstaad, that newest of the fashionable skiing resorts where millionaires' chalets dot the foothills and a helicopter will take you up to the highest ski-runs. I was told the cake was a Valais speciality.

2-layer, freshly baked sponge
cake
1 pint boiled chestnuts
(see page 128)

½ pint whipping cream
2 tablespoons honey
1 teaspoon vanilla extract

Take enough boiled and peeled chestnuts to fill a pint measure. They should be quite tender and well drained. Press through a fine sieve, or put through an electric blender twice. Stir in honey and vanilla and fold in whipped cream.

Sandwich the two layers of cake together with chestnut cream and spread remainder over the top and sides. Chill and serve garnished with thawed and drained frozen strawberries if serving as a dessert. The cake can be cut into four layers and sandwiched together with the cream if desired.

The chestnut cream can also be used over stewed apples, or other fruit.

COFFEE CAKE
(STREUSEL)

1 *pint milk*
1 *oz yeast*
16 *oz plain flour, sifted*
4 *oz salted butter, melted*
10 *oz castor sugar*
3 *eggs*

1 *tablespoon grated lemon*
  rind
1 *teaspoon ground cinnamon*
2 *oz ground almonds*
2 *tablespoons unsalted butter*

Take 2 oz milk from the pint and heat slightly, then dissolve the yeast in it.

Sift half the flour into a large mixing bowl and blend with remainder of milk, stirring to a smooth paste. Add the dissolved yeast to the paste. Set in a warm place and allow to rise until doubled in bulk. Mix in the melted salted butter, lemon rind, eggs, remaining flour and 3 oz castor sugar, mixing thoroughly. Divide the dough in half and pat each into a round about 1-inch thick. Put into two well-greased cake tins, set in a warm place until dough has risen to the edge of the tins.

Cream the unsalted butter with the remaining sugar, and when thoroughly blended work in ground almonds and cinnamon. The mixture should resemble coarse breadcrumbs. Cover the tops of the dough with this mixture. Bake in a moderate oven (350 deg F or No 5) for 45 minutes. Remove from tins immediately. Serve hot or cold, preferably with cups of steaming hot coffee topped with cream.

PEACH AND HAZELNUT CAKE

In the Ticino or Tessin district (it is the same place with the French and Italian version of the name) you could imagine yourself in Italy rather than in Switzerland. The almost flat roofs of the houses are covered with romanesque tiles; pink and blue frontages remind you of Italian villages, and palms and cacti grow in the sunshine.

In many of the Ticino recipes given in this book you will notice that the Italian influence is very strong on the culinary side. This recipe is a good example, using the fruits and nuts which are plentiful in this region, and is one I enjoyed several times in Locarno.

3 eggs
3 oz flour
pinch salt
4½ oz castor sugar
1 teaspoon powdered instant coffee

2 oz ground toasted hazelnuts
3 or 4 ripe peaches
¼ pint cream
honey
little extra flour

Grease an 8-inch sandwich tin and sprinkle with flour, then shake out any surplus. Sift flour, salt and coffee together. Break eggs into a bowl, add sugar, and stand bowl over a pan of hot (but not boiling) water. Beat until thick and fluffy, then remove from heat. Continue whisking until cool, then fold in sifted flour and prepared nuts, keeping the mixture as light as possible. Turn into prepared tin and bake in moderate oven (350 deg F or No 5) for 15 to 20 minutes. When cool, split through middle and sandwich together again with sliced peaches mixed with whipped cream and honey to taste.

EASTER CAKE

This cake is always made at Easter time by the house-wives and pastrycooks of Zürich.

FOR PASTRY :

8 *oz flour*	2 *oz castor sugar*
4 *oz butter*	1 *tablespoon water*
1 *egg*	*pinch salt*

FOR FILLING :

1 *pint milk*	*grated rind* ½ *lemon*
pinch salt	¼ *teaspoon cinnamon*
3½ *oz groats*	3½ *oz ground almonds*
2 *oz butter*	3 *oz sultanas*
2 *oz sugar*	¾ *cup sour cream*
4 *eggs, separated*	

Make the pastry by sieving flour and salt into a basin, then rub butter in lightly with tips of fingers until mixture resembles fine breadcrumbs. Add sugar, and beat egg with water, adding just enough to mix to a firm dough. Turn on to a floured board and pat out into a rectangle to fit into a deep baking tin.

For the filling, boil the milk then stir in groats and salt, and simmer until thick, stirring occasionally. Cream butter and sugar, and beat in egg yolks, add peel, almonds, cinnamon and sour cream and mix with cooked groats. Beat egg whites until stiff and fold into filling. Spread this mixture over pastry and cook in a moderate oven (350 deg F or No 5) until pastry is golden and filling cooked.

SPICED HONEY BISCUITS
(HONIGSKUCHEN)

Delicious little biscuits are made all over Switzerland, many of them flavoured with honey. These are a speciality of the district of Appenzell.

1 egg	½ teaspoon cinnamon
2 dessertspoons milk	¼ teaspoon ground cloves
½ cup sugar	¼ teaspoon grated nutmeg
1 cup honey	1 lb flour

Stand honey over boiling water until liquid. Beat egg, milk and sugar together, then add honey. Sift flour and spices together and blend into honey mixture a little at a time until you have a firm dough. Stand for 3–4 hours. When ready to bake roll out dough about ½-inch thick and cut into 3-inch rounds. Place on greased baking slides and bake in moderate oven (350 deg F or No 5) until golden brown.

ALMOND KNOTS
(MANDELBRETZEL)

4 oz butter	8 oz ground almonds
2 large eggs	almond essence
7 oz flour	1 egg for glazing

Cream the butter well, then beat in eggs one at a time. Gradually beat in flour and ground almonds, then the essence until mixture is firm. Knead lightly and roll out about ¼-inch thick. Cut into narrow strips about 6-inches long and carefully tie into lover's knots or bows. Place on greased oven slide, brush over with beaten egg, and bake in moderate oven (350 deg F or No 5) for 8–10 minutes, until golden brown.

BASLE CINNAMON BISCUITS
(BASLER LECKERLI)

These cinnamon flavoured biscuits are a speciality of
Basle, and are always made for every festive occasion.

¾ lb honey	4 oz almonds, shredded
¾ lb sugar	4 oz hazelnuts, chopped
½ oz cinnamon	4 oz candied orange and lemon
1 lb plain flour	peel, shredded
½ cup kirsch	

Cook, honey, sugar and spices together until melted
then remove from heat. Add peel and half the flour, nuts
and kirsch, mixing well. Now knead in remainder of
flour. Spread mixture over a greased and floured
baking tin, about ¼-inch thick. Sprinkle lightly with
flour and bake in a moderate oven (No 5 or 350 deg F)
for about 20 minutes or until biscuit turns brown. Turn
out of tin and with a sharp knife cut the leckerli in
halves through the middle thickness before it gets cold.
Brush off the flour, and cover with plain sugar icing.
Cut into pieces and store in an airtight tin.

CHEESE STICKS
(BÂTONNETS AU FROMAGE)

Delicious to serve with drinks before dinner.

2 oz grated Sbrinz cheese	2 tablespoons butter
2 oz grated Emmental cheese	1 large egg
3 oz flour	salt, pepper and paprika

Rub butter into flour, add cheese, seasonings and lightly beaten egg and blend to a firm paste, adding a little water if necessary. Chill for a little time, then roll out and cut into thin sticks. Bake in a moderate oven until crisp and golden.

HORSE SHOES
(FERS À CHEVAL)

These can be served hot or cold, and are good for a buffet party or to pack in a picnic basket.

flaky pastry   *yolk of an egg*
grated Emmental cheese   *paprika*

Roll out pastry about ⅛-inch thick into three equal size rectangles. Sprinkle one rectangle thickly with cheese and dust lightly with paprika. Cover with another rectangle of pastry and repeat layer of cheese and paprika, then cover with third piece of pastry. Roll lightly with rolling pin, keeping shape of pastry, and cut into strips about 1-inch by 6-inches. Twist into shape of a horse-shoe, brush over lightly with beaten egg yolk and lightly sprinkle with grated cheese and paprika. Bake in a very hot oven (425 deg F or No 8) until golden brown.

ALMOND FINGERS

6 *oz ground almonds*   ½ *teaspoon cinnamon*
6 *oz icing sugar*   1 *egg white*

ICING :
2 *teaspoons flour*   1 *egg white*
2 *oz icing sugar*

Make the biscuits by sieving sugar and cinnamon into ground almonds then making into a stiff paste with the lightly beaten egg white. Knead until smooth, then roll out about ¼-inch thick.

Sift icing sugar and flour together and blend with egg white to right consistency for icing. Spread over the almond mixture and cut into fingers. Place on a greased and floured tin and bake in moderately hot oven (375 deg F or No 6) until golden brown and crisp, about 20 minutes. Cool on a rack.

HAZELNUT CAKES

These come from Eastern Switzerland, where the pastrycooks make most tempting cakes and pastries with nuts and fruits.

6 *oz finely ground hazelnuts*   1 *egg white*
4 *oz ground almonds*   ¼ *teaspoon vanilla essence*
6 *oz brown sugar*   *white icing*
1 *dessertspoon potato flour*   *whole blanched nuts*

Mix ground nuts, sugar and flour together and add just enough lightly beaten egg white to bind mixture together. Add essence. Spread on wafer paper in circles about ¼-inch thick and 4 inches in diameter, and flatten edges with a damp knife. Bake in a moderate oven (350 deg F or No 5) until crisp and lightly browned, cool on a rack and then ice and garnish with nuts.

APRICOT BRANDY

As mentioned in another part of this book, excellent wines are one of the products Switzerland is very proud of, but the housewife also likes to make her own fruit-flavoured brandies, such as these.

Choose 12 large ripe apricots and cut them into small pieces, then put into a bottle with ½ lb sugar. Crack the stones and extract the kernels, then crush them and add to the apricots. Add 1 pint or more of brandy and shake well together. Cork the bottle securely and store in a cool, dark place for a month, shaking the bottle at frequent intervals. After a month, strain off the liquor and re-bottle.

CHERRY BRANDY

Although kirsch, the cherry-flavoured liquor, is famous as a Swiss product, this home-made version is also very popular.

Use only sound, ripe, dark cherries. Wash and cut stalks to within ¼-inch of the fruit, then with a skewer, prick cherries in several places. For 2 lbs cherries allow

6 oz castor sugar, and put alternate layers of cherries and sugar in a wide-mouthed bottle. Add 1 pint or more of good brandy, making sure cherries are covered. Cork bottle securely, and store in a cool, dark place for at least 2 months (three months is better if you have patience enough), shaking at intervals. When time is up, strain off the liquor and re-bottle.

BLACK CHERRY JAM
(KIRSCHENMARMELADE)

There are many charming old villages around the shores of Lake Lucerne with accommodation for visitors, usually in inns rather than hotels, and all the better for that. If you choose one overlooking the lake, you can have breakfast in the sunshine with a view of the blue waters, and enjoy a good pot of coffee, a basket of freshly baked rolls or croissants, lavish home-made dairy butter, and black cherry jam – far better than the toast and marmalade of an English breakfast, in my opinion.

And when you go home, look for some sweet black cherries when they are in season and make some of the luscious jam to remind you of Swiss breakfasts.

4 *lb stoned, ripe black cherries*   *cherry-stone kernels*
1 *lb sugar*   1 *gill red currant juice*
1 *teaspoon powdered cinnamon*

Prepare the red currant juice by boiling crushed red currants without water until soft, then rubbing through a sieve. Add to stoned cherries, sugar, and cinnamon and boil gently until jam thickens when tested on a cold saucer. Add a few kernels for extra flavour. Pour into warm sterilized jars and seal.

The cherries should be ripe and sweet, without blemishes, or the jam will not keep.

PEACH PRESERVE

Peel the peaches by dropping into boiling water for a minute, after which the skin comes off easily. Cut in halves and remove stones. Rub the peach pulp through a sieve, then measure pulp and add $\frac{3}{4}$ lb sugar to each pound of pulp. Boil until the mixture turns thick like a paste, then turn into hot sterilized jars and seal. This is very good as a cake or pie filling.

Or it can be spread in a flat dish about $\frac{1}{4}$-inch thick and put into a slightly warm oven or in the sun until paste is dry and firm enough to turn over to dry on other side. Cut into squares and wrap in squares of greaseproof paper, then store in airtight tins. This makes a delicious sweet and is sometimes served with squares of cheese.

PEACH AND RASPBERRY JAM

This recipe was given to me by a housewife in the Valais district, which is known as Switzerland's orchard country.

2 lb stoned peaches $\frac{1}{4}$ pint water
2 lb raspberries   3 lb sugar

Peel the peaches as directed above and remove stones before weighing them. Crack the stones to obtain the kernels. Cut peaches into slices, wash and pick over the raspberries, but drain them well. Put fruit and water into pan with the kernels and cook gently until tender. Add sugar and stir until completely dissolved. Boil for 15 minutes, stirring at intervals, then test for setting. If ready, pour into warm sterilized jars and cover.

MIXED SALTED VEGETABLES

This is the way many country housewives preserve vegetables for use during the winter when fresh ones are unobtainable. In this way they are available for sauces, salads, soups, etc. The vegetables can be mixed in proportions to suit yourself. They should be well washed in cold water to remove salt before using.

Take ½ lb each of carrots, celeriac (or celery), leeks, cabbage, onions, and some parsley, chives and celery leaves. Cut chives with a pair of scissors and put other vegetables through the mincer, using a coarse blade. Mix with 3 oz cooking salt, pack into sterilized jars leaving room at the top for a 1-inch layer of salt. Cover with two or three thicknesses of greaseproof paper tied firmly. These should keep for 1 year unopened.

TOMATOES IN VINEGAR

Use firm but ripe tomatoes, and put those of the same size in sterilized jars together. Fill jars nearly to the top with good quality vinegar, making sure the tomatoes are covered. Pour off vinegar into an enamel saucepan and bring to the boil. Cool, then fill jars to about 1-inch of the top, then pour in a 1-inch layer of olive oil. Cover with several thicknesses of paper and tie firmly. These will keep well for months. Wash well in cold water before using.

❧❧❧❧❧❧❧❧❧❧❧❧❧❧❧❧❧❧❧❧

EXTRA DISHES

❧❧❧❧❧❧❧❧❧❧❧❧❧❧❧❧❧❧❧❧

BIRCHERMÜESLI

This is a very popular breakfast dish, not only in Switzerland, but in many places where the name of Dr Bircher-Benner is familiar. This famous doctor from Zürich advocated the use of uncooked cereals, fruit, vegetables and other natural health foods, and he has many followers all over the world. This breakfast dish is one of his most famous creations. It is also delicious as a dessert to finish a meal.

For each person:

1 *tablespoon oatmeal*
3 *tablespoons water*
1 *tablespoon cream* WITH
  1 *teaspoon honey* OR
  1 *tablespoon sweetened*
    condensed milk

juice of ½ lemon
1 *large apple or same quantity*
  of other fresh fruit
1 *tablespoon chopped nuts*

Soak oatmeal overnight in water. In the morning peel apple and grate it, mixing at once with lemon juice to prevent discolouring. Blend with soaked oatmeal, condensed milk or cream and honey, then sprinkle chopped nuts on top. Serve at once.

When fresh fruit is not available seeded raisins or pre-soaked prunes may be used.

GNOCCHI
(SEMOLINA)

There are two kinds of gnocchi served in the Ticino district, this one made with semolina, or the one on page 47 made with potatoes. Both make very good meatless dishes with cheese, or they can be served with a sauce of tomatoes and ham. These amounts will serve 4.

1 *pint milk*
4 *oz fine semolina*
2 *oz butter*

4 *oz grated cheese*
1 *beaten egg*
salt, pepper and ground nutmeg

Heat the milk until nearly boiling, add seasonings and gradually add the semolina, stirring all the time to get a smooth mixture. Cook gently until the mixture is quite thick, remove from heat and stir in 1 oz butter and 1 oz cheese. Mix well then beat in egg, blending well. Cook for about a minute over low heat, but do not get too hot. Pour the mixture into an oiled shallow dish in a layer about ¼-inch deep, and leave until cold and set firmly.

Cut into rounds with a cutter about 1½-inch diameter and arrange in overlapping layers in a buttered oven-proof dish. Sprinkle with remainder of cheese and dot with remaining butter, put into a hot oven (425 deg F or No 8) for a few minutes until cheese has melted into a golden sauce on top. Serve at once.

This dish can be varied by adding a finely chopped onion to the semolina as it cooks, or chopped ham can be added with the cheese to the mixture. I have also eaten it with a layer of peeled, sliced tomatoes as the first and last layer in the dish, with the circles in the middle, and the cheese and butter on top forming a sauce.

GRANDMA'S SPAGHETTI
(SPAGHETTI A LA MODE DE GRAND'MÈRE)

This is a real farmhouse spaghetti from the Grisons area, and it makes a tasty and very filling dish.

4 oz fat bacon, in one piece	2 tablespoons butter
4 oz ham	spaghetti
4 oz stale bread	

Cut the bacon and ham in ½-inch cubes. Remove crusts from bread and cut in cubes the same size. Melt the butter in a thick pan and sauté the bacon and ham until crisp, then add bread cubes and sauté until golden brown and crisp, turning to brown evenly. Have the spaghetti cooking in boiling, salted water for 10 minutes, or until tender but not mushy. Drain well and add remaining ingredients, tossing to blend. Serve at once.

PASTA SHELLS AND PEAS

Another pasta recipe, this one from the Ticino, using those very decorative pasta shells and served with a green sauce. Other forms of fancy pasta can be used in the same way.

8 oz pasta shells	¼ cup olive oil
2½ cups cooked, fresh peas	¼ cup melted butter
1 cup finely chopped onion	1 cup finely chopped parsley
2 cloves garlic, finely chopped	salt and pepper

Cook shells in boiling, salted water until tender, about 10 minutes, then drain well. Sauté onion and garlic in butter and oil for 10 minutes. Add other ingredients to pan, turning over heat for 1 minute, then pour into greased casserole, cover and bake 15 minutes in moderate oven (350 deg F or No 5).

POLENTA

In the Italian part of Switzerland much of the food has an Italian savour and inspiration. Butter-yellow polenta is an important item in the everyday food of this region, as it is in Northern Italy. Made of yellow maize flour, it is served in a variety of ways as a complete dish, or as an accompaniment to meat dishes instead of potatoes. There are two grades of polenta, coarse or finely ground, and they can be bought in most Continental stores in England.

½ lb fine polenta	1½ pints salted water

Bring water to a rolling boil and pour in polenta, stirring with a wooden spoon until a thick, smooth paste. Cook slowly for 20 minutes, stirring frequently.

It can be eaten at once with melted butter and grated cheese, or turned out on a marble slab or large platter to get cold, then it is cut into squares, dipped in egg and breadcrumbs and fried until crisp and brown.

Or put a layer of polenta into a buttered ovenproof dish, cover with a layer of Gruyère cheese (either grated or sliced), a little melted butter and a sprinkle of pepper. Repeat these layers, depending on number to be served, finishing with a layer of cheese and butter. Put into a hot oven and cook until bubbling and top nicely browned. This can also be made with sliced tomatoes between the layers of polenta and cheese.

SPAETZLI

1 *lb flour*   2 *eggs*
¾ *pint mixed milk and water*   1 *teaspoon salt*

Warm the milk and water and stir into flour, stirring until smooth, then beat in eggs, beating the batter until bubbles form. Have ready a large saucepan of boiling salted water. Drop the batter in small portions from the point of a spoon into the boiling water. Do not attempt to cook too many at one time. As the spaetzli rise to the top of the water they are cooked, and should be lifted from the water with a perforated spoon at once and placed on a hot plate.

They can be served at once with hot butter and grated cheese over the top, or covered with fried onions as a main dish. They are also served instead of potatoes with many game and meat dishes.

In the Glaris district housewives add finely chopped and drained spinach to the spaetzli mixture (reducing the amount of milk and water) and serve them with melted butter and grated Schabzieger cheese, under the name of Knopflis.

In the Canton Thurgau they add finely minced liver to the original recipe, again reducing the liquid used, but cooking them in the same way.

INDEX